The Teacher-Parent Partnership
In the Primary Grades

Pathways to Communication and Cooperation

Angela Maiers

Illustrated by Darcy Tom

Rigby Best Teachers Press

An imprint of Rigby

DEDICATION

This book is dedicated with deepest love and gratitude to my grandparents Charles and Gladys. Their love, trust, and encouragement continue to surround and support me as a teacher, wife, and mother.

Acknowledgments

No writing project is ever done in isolation. This book is a reflection of the insights and influences of many. I would like to acknowledge some of the people who have helped me see this project to completion.

First, I would like to thank my students and their parents who joined me in the discovery process and willingly shared their insights and observations. Special thanks to my research partner and friend, Dr. Robert Nistler, whose enthusiasm, confidence, and faith in me propelled me forward. My deepest appreciation to my friend and colleague John Slagle for his clear, original thinking and willingness to share. I want to thank the editorial and publishing team at Rigby who were supportive of and patient with this first-time book author.

Of course many thanks to my friends and family, especially my mother who was a constant voice of reason and support, and to my children, Abby and Ryan, for all their wonderful distractions. And to Bob, my husband, thank you for your encouragement and carrying so much of the load while I worked to complete this book.

For more information about other books from Rigby Best Teachers Press, please contact Rigby at 800-822-8661 or **www.rigby.com**

Editor: *Roberta Dempsey*
Executive Editor: *Laura Strom*
Designer: *Nancy Rudd*
Design Project Manager: *Tom Sjoerdsma*
Cover Illustrator: *Robert Gunn*
Interior Illustrator: *Darcy Tom*

06 05 04 03 02
10 9 8 7 6 5 4 3

Printed in the United States of America.

ISBN 0-7635-7340-X

Preface

To share with you part of the *how* and *why* this book came about, I will begin with two entries from a journal I kept as a part of my research in family literacy. The first entry was written after a hot summer day in July. I had just completed a day of home visits in hopes of recruiting parents to take part in a new parent involvement program I had developed for my first-grade classroom.

July 16, 1996: Home Visit Journal Entry–Summer Program Recruitment

Today I visited four families, but it was the last visit of the day that has stayed with me. I met Alec and his son Marcus. They are living in a small, one-bedroom apartment with Alec's cousin until they can find a place of their own. Marcus's mother is in jail. Alec recently found work with a local construction company. Alec is raising his son alone. I introduced myself to Marcus and told him that I would be his teacher for the coming year. I shared with Alec my hopes and dreams for a new program I was implementing in my first-grade classroom, which would involve parents in a new way. He closed his arms tightly and said he would not be participating in any "program." He explained his busy work schedule and the responsibilities he faced as a single father. Although he listened politely to the details about the program, his guard was up. He seemed unresponsive to what I had to say. Finally, he stated that his experience at Marcus's previous school had been frustrating and upsetting for both of them.

I wanted this year to be different for them. I asked Alec to meet me at school any time that first week so we could help Marcus make a smooth transition to his new school. There was no answer. Though it was obvious from the way he looked at Marcus and referred to him throughout the conversation that Alec loved his son very much, I still wondered if he would come.

October 1998: Journal entry written after Alec was asked to speak, as a part of a parent panel, to a graduate course I teach on "Creating Family School Partnerships"

As Alec sat there today, so proud and confident, my mind drifted back to that summer day in July when I visited his apartment trying to convince him of the benefits of parent involvement. It took all I had to keep my composure when he talked. I was beaming with pride, in awe of how much he had grown in the time we had worked together. He did come to our first meeting, and from that point on, he never stopped being involved.

Now he is sharing his story with others. He points his finger to the audience of graduate students who are eager to hear from parents their thoughts and insights about parent involvement. He begins, "You teachers, parent involvement is the most important thing you can do in your classrooms. It is

everything. She got me to come and you have to get your parents there, too. My parents weren't involved. I was abused. They were not there for me, but I am here for him.

If those powerful words were not enough for my students to hear, Marcus sat across the room looking at his father with great admiration and respect. Their eyes were locked on one another. The room was silent as Alec became emotional. Alec apologized for breaking down. He paused and continued: "I want to see him graduate. I did not graduate. My boy," he said, and his eyes filled with tears, "he is the most important thing in the world."

I wanted so badly to race up there and give him a hug, but I had to continue the facilitation of the panel. Another parent reached over and gently patted Alec on the back for support. I commented with a heartfelt "Thank you for sharing." Inside I was bursting. He had given so much to make Marcus's life better than his own. My admiration and respect for him was so immense.

He thanked the panel and me for giving him the opportunity to share his insights. He repeated several times how important and special it made him feel to be a part of this group and to help teachers work more successfully with the parents in their classrooms. It was me who should be thanking him. My class listened to his words and saw the love in his eyes as he looked at his son. When he left that day, he told me that he had lost his job, and they were moving on again to find work and a place to live. He had already made plans to go and meet with Marcus's new teacher. Won't she be the lucky one!

He hugged me and thanked me for all that I had done for him and his son. I gave him my address and asked him to send me an invitation to Marcus's graduation. I will wait and expect a special piece of mail in 10 years or so. This was a day that I will never forget. It made all the extra time and effort worth every minute and more. Thank you, Alec, for all that you have taught me about being a teacher, parent, and friend.

Although I cannot recreate that special day in words, this journal entry illustrates the powerful and lasting impact working closely with families can have on everyone involved. It is a small window into understanding the vital role families play in the education of their children.

To me, the heart of any family literacy or parent involvement program is the relationship that is built with families such as the one I had built with Alec and Marcus. Beneath the activities and programs lie the relationships, which become the foundational stepping stones along the partnership pathway. Partnerships must begin with a genuine respect and acknowledgment that parents are their child's first and foremost teachers. For these reciprocal relationships to flourish, time, space, and support must be invested in creating an environment.

In my speaking and writing I am asked to describe the "population" of children

and families with whom I learned. From a statistician's point of view, my classroom community existed in an urban, inner-city school where 100 percent of the families qualified for free or reduced lunches, mobility rates were high, and the population largely comprised minority students living at or below the poverty level. When my parents were asked to describe the population of our classroom community, they commented with such statements as "It is a place I feel secure," "It is a place of learning," "It is a place where I feel valued and welcome," and "It is like a family to me." It is from this perspective that my work with families has developed. I have learned that it is not how much money you have or the culture you were raised in that makes a parent more or less involved, but rather the value that each family places on literacy that becomes the focus. Diversity in our classroom community was looked at as an opportunity for learning, sharing, and growth.

My official study ended after those two years, but my appreciation and amazement for all that I learned from the families involved still continues. The families in my program broke through many barriers and defied every stereotype bestowed upon them. Their belief in and commitment to the children's education was amazing. The times we were together were not fancy and cost little money. I invited them into our "first-grade world." Every other Friday morning, parents came in to be a part of a family literacy group. For two years, they spent time at school engaging in multiple literacy activities with their children. Through journaling, cooking, reading, and writing, everyone learned. Their dedication and support serve as a timeless reminder of the potential and possibilities for successful home-school partnerships.

As I work with teachers across the country trying to answer the question of how to get more parents involved, my message is very simple. True partnerships are built on trusting relationships over time. Each week you are together, each activity you share, each conversation you have, and each barrier you acknowledge and break down puts you one step closer along the pathway.

This is a book for all teachers who believe working with families can and will make a difference. It is written as a place to begin conversation—conversation about redefining parent involvement as a school and in your own classrooms; conversation about the role parents can and should play in their child's education; conversation about tools and techniques to get all families involved. The activities I share are ones that I used to help me in forming partnerships with the families in my classroom. It is my hope that they can and will serve as a tool and guide to help you make those important connections with families upon which the foundations of partnerships are built.

True partnerships are built on trusting relationships over time. Each week you are together, each activity you share, each conversation you have, and each barrier you acknowledge and break down puts you one step closer along the pathway.

I believe that parents are the most powerful, underutilized source of information and knowledge you can find—a great untapped resource. Families can and do provide us with a vast reservoir of talent, energy, and insight. When you invite them to join in, your classroom will never be the same!

This book represents the winding down of my journey with families. It has been an exciting and eventful road. In writing this book, I have enjoyed reflecting on and sharing with you some of the ideas and activities that have brought me closer to the families in my classroom.

Remember that you are your own best resource. Only you will know how to relate to the unique group of families and children you will work with. Embrace their eagerness to support you, their knowledge, and willingness to do what is best for their children.

Parent involvement is one of the toughest issues facing teachers and schools today. The road to partnership will not be without rocks and bumps, but I promise you that the time and energy invested in smoothing out the course will be well spent. Greet the challenges with knowledge, openness, and respect for what families have to offer. Good luck, and enjoy the journey!

Contents

Introduction

Although it has been said many times, it bears repeating: parents are a child's first teachers. There is no formula or best recipe for school reform, but the one consistent element that contributes to more successful children and more successful schools is parent involvement. When our focus is on improving student achievement and moving schools to the next level, partnership with families is not just important but a crucial element of change. It is my hope that the ideas shared in this book will be of use to you as teachers and parents on a successful journey toward effective partnership. The road to partnership involves examining the pathway on many levels.

Chapter 1 examines the many benefits of parent involvement, characteristics of successful partnership, and some potential barriers that may inhibit full involvement. This chapter will provide you with suggestions and activities to use in including all families in the learning partnership.

No parent involvement program is effective without a high level of communication, trust, and respect between teachers and parents. The importance of communication with parents does not make the task easy. **Chapter 2** provides tips and handouts to help support you in this process and inspire you to develop and nurture a deeper, richer level of communication with families. Use the strategies to help with planning, scheduling, and maintaining regular, informative communication with the families in your classroom.

A strong home-school connection is essential when building a good environment for young children. We want parents to support us in the process of extending and developing their child as a lifelong literacy learner. **Chapter 3** shares with parents the many ways we support this development at school and offers concrete, specific ways parents can support and encourage that development at home.

Learning at home and school is the focus of the next chapter. The letters in **Chapter 4** contain suggestions of activities parents can do with their children at home. The activities help families understand that children learn through a multitude of experiences. Each letter links classroom learning to additional learning opportunities at home.

Parents are boundless in their information and insight into their child's development and learning. **Chapter 5** deals with one of the most central times of this information sharing: parent-teacher conferences. All aspects of conferences are addressed, from planning and preparation to dealing with potentially difficult situations.

Children learn best when activities are meaningful to them. Games provide this opportunity; playing games is a wonderful

way for children to share time with family members, to have fun, and to learn. The games in **Chapter 6** were designed for parents to use as they experience literacy everywhere they go: driving a car, taking a bus, or walking around the block. Literacy abounds when parents and children spend time together. These literacy games can become shared moments of fun and learning.

Cooking is a great way to involve families and show them the fun that is embedded in learning. The unique recipes in **Chapter 7** have been especially created and designed so that children and parents can read, write, and cook their way through learning skills in math, science, and literacy. The focus of each activity is the learning that accompanies cooking and the closeness fostered by the shared experience.

Chapter 8 presents a workshop approach. The workshop environment provides time for ongoing interaction and support while engaging children and their families in an active learning process at school. This leads to positive learning results and nurtures a commitment to lifelong learning from both parents and children. Sample workshop activities, agendas, and ideas are presented.

The **Resources** at the back of the book include lists of new books, publications, articles, videos, and Internet sources that make information about students, parents, and school partnership accessible.

The information in this book will give you a sense of the possibilities available for partnership. Each chapter offers ideas and insights into creating the partnership that will work best for your classroom. As the title suggests, a plan can take many forms and shapes; create your own route. Use the ideas as a springboard for conversation and thought. Let them serve in helping you create your own unique ways of connecting with the families with whom you work.

1 Paving the Way

Betty Shockley, Barbara Michalove, and JoBeth Allen, in their book *Engaging Families* (1998), write eloquently about the creation of family school partnerships: "Programs are implemented; partnerships are developed. Programs are adopted; partnerships are constructed." Unfortunately, there is no blueprint for creating the ideal partnership. Scholars and researchers alike have described data that supports irrefutably that schools that collaborate effectively with parents are more successful all around. These schools are places where parents, teachers, and students are more successful and happy.

Because each school is different, there is no one set model of practice that would make partnership with families a guarantee. There are, however, some basic principles throughout the literature that schools that work successfully with parents share. If the staff, administration, and families subscribe to many or most of these principles, their attempts to increase parent involvement can be greatly improved.

Principle 1: Create a climate in the school that is welcoming, helpful, and friendly.

What Can I Do?

- Place signs around the school and classrooms welcoming parents and visitors.
- Create a sign or map directing parents to the school office.
- Design a special area for parents: a lounge, resource center, or designated table for materials and information display.
- Have a plan in place to welcome and orient new families.

Principle 2: Communicate, communicate, communicate.

What Can I Do?

It is vital that communication be ongoing and occur in multiple ways:

- Send information home that helps parents understand school programs, policy, and their child's progress in a clear, understandable format.
- Make time in your day to communicate with families. This can be before or after

school; it can be time to make phone calls or to send notes home about a student.

- Keep a record of both the nature and type of parent contacts. This will help you monitor how and when you are making those needed connections with families.

Principle 3: Treat parents as true partners in the educational process.

What Can I Do?

- View parents as an invaluable resource, a new window into understanding your students.
- Seek assistance from parents in many ways, both when problems arise and for their special talents and knowledge.
- Request a formal meeting with parents at least twice during the year to update them on progress and goals in their child's growth.

Principle 4: Try to involve all families, not just those most easily reached.

What Can I Do?

- Getting every family involved is not a simple task. Special attention is needed for many families and situations.
- Know your families. Make a list of possible barriers they may face that could hinder their involvement. Is it transportation concerns? Child care availability? Feelings of insecurity or uneasiness about coming to school? Work or scheduling conflicts? Language or cultural issues?
- Do not assume that parents aren't concerned or caring because they appear uninvolved. It is important to investigate before making judgments.
- Ask for assistance to overcome possible barriers: flex time for scheduling, a translator, money for child care, and transportation to special school events.
- Always begin on the assumption that all parents want the best for their child and really want to work with you.

Principle 5: Develop and promote your philosophy of partnership.

What Can I Do?

- Actively express to parents how vital you see them to be.
- Investigate your school philosophy and administrative stand on how to involve parents.
- Talk with other staff members about how they work successfully with families, sharing ideas and support.
- Work with parents both in and out of your classroom. Try sitting in on a parent organization meeting or advisory council meeting.

Creating Home-School Partnerships

When parents and families get more personally involved in the educational process, their children do better in school and grow up to be more successful in life. This sounds like common sense, so much so that we take for granted the power of such relations when we look for ways to improve student attitude and achievement. Parental involvement is one of the most overlooked aspects of education in the United States. The fact is that many parents and teachers don't realize how important and easy it is to get involved in their child's learning.

Use the following pages of information to disseminate the positive outcomes of working as a team with families. This information can be put on posters, used in newsletters, or shared at workshops and in conversation. The more you share and celebrate the potential successes of a parent partnership, the more you will increase the possibilities of parents and teachers committing time, energy, and effort to partnership formation.

When schools and families work together . . .

- Children's grades and test scores improve.
- Parent-child relations improve.
- The school is better able to understand the needs and concerns of families.
- Parents understand what is happening at school and are more likely to participate.
- The community feels more of a connection to the school.
- The atmosphere for parents, students, and teachers is more positive and supportive.
- The sense of community grows as relationships between teachers and parents, parents and parents, and students and parents is strengthened.

Everybody wins when parents and schools work together!

Parent Involvement: Creating a Path

As you find your pathway to building a successful partnership with families, it may be helpful to look at the journey as having the following levels:

1. **Examining My Role:** Self-assessment is a necessity. Looking closely at how your beliefs, wishes, and understandings of parent involvement affect your role in the parent involvement process is an important first step on the pathway to partnership.

2. **Examining Barriers:** Acknowledging and understanding potential barriers that may affect your partnership with families is an important first step in overcoming potential blocks in the pathway.

3. **Reaching Out:** It is important to consider and explore every tool that will assist in your efforts to reach out and make connections with all families.

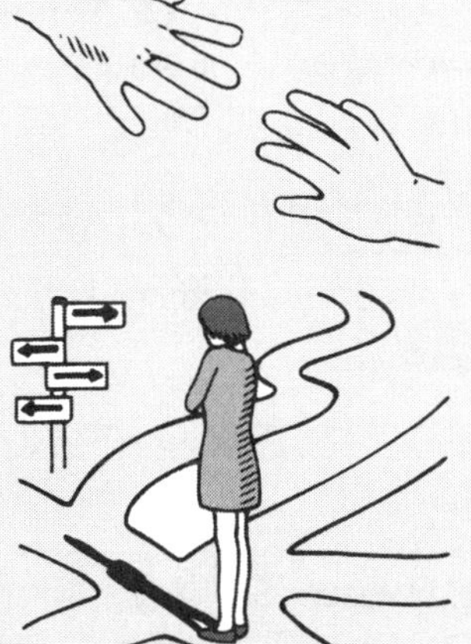

4. **Where Do I Go from Here?:** Now you can begin planning for future successful involvement opportunities.

Examining My Role

Many schools have a small group of parents who are there much or most of the time. They are the acknowledged parent leaders from within the school and your own classrooms. Although it is important to support and encourage their good work and effort, there is also a body of families who can be untapped resources. If your personal or school goal is to increase parent participation, then your outreach needs to target all parents. This is no easy task; in our busy day, time is a precious commodity. Trying to find time to send one note home is often hard, and with many families, reaching out in only one way may not be enough. Use some of the following activities and exercises to determine who needs to be reached and narrow the focus of your efforts. Once you have examined some of these questions, you can begin to look at successful strategies for reaching out to all parents in your classroom.

1. Are there any roadblocks that may keep families away? (child care, transportation, language issues) If so, how do you address them in your classroom and school?
2. Are you reaching out to families in multiple ways? (newsletters, home visits, phone calls)
3. Is your communication frequent and ongoing?
4. Do you access and use parent input? How do you do so? (interviews, questionnaires, surveys)
5. Do families have clear expectations as to what they can and should do to help their child have a successful school year?
6. Have you established a comfortable, trusting atmosphere that encourages a partnership to flourish? Do parents openly and freely come to you for advice and support?
7. Do you know your families? In what ways do you get to know their beliefs, expectations, and customs better?
8. How often do you communicate with them? (monthly, weekly, daily)
9. What types of communication do you most frequently use?
10. Are the activities you plan worthwhile and meaningful?
11. Are you creative, sensitive, and responsible to families' needs and situations?

Examining Barriers

If parent involvement is such a good thing, why then is it so difficult to achieve? Most often it is not lack of interest that prohibits a successful partnership, but there may be barriers that cause potential isolation and inhibit parents from being involved and teachers from reaching out more. Here we will examine those barriers from both the teacher's and family's perspective so that you may overcome as many barriers as possible that stand in your way of having a thriving partnership with your families.

Research in parent involvement has taught us that barriers to getting parents involved can be overcome. The first step is recognition and understanding. Changing demographics and diverse family situation make the task of getting all parents involved in the same way very difficult. By expanding our views of parent involvement and believing that all parents want the best for their child, you can open up many new relationships with the families you reach.

Following are some of the most common barriers for both parents and teachers, along with some possible suggestions and solutions to consider in overcoming them.

1. The Changing Family

When planning parent involvement activities, it may be helpful to view families in the broadest sense. The family structure in the United States is changing at a rate faster than ever before. A variety of new words describe today's modern families: extended, blended, mutigenerational, multilingual, single parent, dual-role. The list can go on. If we are to involve all families, we need to be aware of differences when planning programs for people in all of these groups. Research indicates that there is no one best program or way to handle parent involvement. What seems to work best is for parents to be involved in many different roles over time. It is more important that parent involvement initiatives be well planned, comprehensive, and long-lasting rather than that they take on a prescribed type or form.

2. Time

Time is an issue for us all. There is never enough time to do all that is required of us. Often school philosophies and administrative actions do not support working with parents. Teachers rarely receive either staffing arrangements or the compensatory time that is needed to respond with the flexibility parent involvement requires. As with anything you do, you must weigh the benefit of the task to the time required. Flexibility is key here. When you schedule a program, workshop, conference, or appointment, be sure to inquire about families' schedules ahead of time so that you can offer times that are convenient. Offering several options increases the opportunity for them

to be involved. Time is precious, and parents will come if they feel it will be useful and beneficial.

Here are some ways to maneuver around time as a barrier. If working together is perceived as important to parents and teachers, time will be dedicated to the goal. Try scheduling contacts with one or two families each day. These individualized, daily contacts are more effective at building partnership relations than large, full-scale events one or two times during the year. This can be a phone call or a quick note. The key to success is setting aside 10 minutes in your lesson plans so you are thinking about continuous contacts. Invite parents in during the school day to help or work with the children. This will avoid additional time added to your day. Ask your administration for possibilities of extra compensation or time available to extend your contact efforts with families.

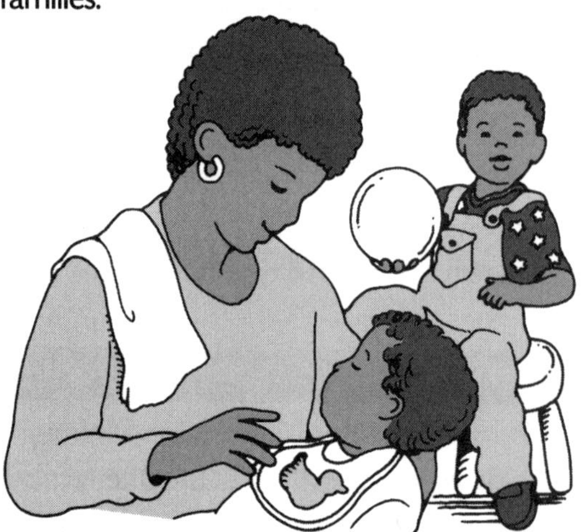

3. Child Care

Parents who don't have intermittent child care available will often not get involved. If a program is offered that requires parents only, then it may be wise to find an available room in the school for child care. Parents could rotate in staffing the room or hire outside help. If you share with your administrator how important it is for parents to meet with you, he or she may be willing to help.

4. Expectations

In many cases it is not that parents are not willing to help but that they are unsure of how or what to contribute. Just as you set up expectations with your students, you must do so for parents. Let them know your policy for involvement. How much, when, how? Can they drop in anytime or do you have days arranged for observations and visits? Conduct a talent survey of the parents and think of ways you can use the parents' many talents and gifts. Encourage them to share their careers, hobbies, and pets. (See page 33.)

5. Unclear About the System

Parents may not know or understand fully school and classroom policies. Each teacher has his or her own way of running a successful classroom. It is important that you communicate clearly to parents, both verbally and in writing, preferably in a parent handbook, where information is easily accessible. You may want to go over points in the handbook with parents at conferences or "back to school" night. What seems clear to you may not be clear to parents. This personal contact can clear up any misinformation and communication from the start.

6. Language and Cultural Differences

Our classrooms are becoming increasingly diverse. Often we are teaching students who represent a different culture, religion, or background than ourselves. If the parents of the students in your classroom do not read or speak English, then you need to have printed materials translated so they have equal access to the information. You may need to arrange for an interpreter at conferences and meeting times. It is important to be sensitive to other cultures,

values, attitudes, and views of school. Learn what you can about the customs and traditions of all groups represented in your school. Your families can be a great resource of knowledge for you. They will appreciate your eagerness and willingness to understand and learn from them.

7. Feeling Unvalued

This may not be a conscious gesture on the teacher's part, but many parents believe that their opinions and feelings are unimportant and that the teacher is "above" their intellectual level. These feelings often stem from a parent's negative experience with a previous school or teacher. Often these parents are less trusting of schools and may be reluctant about becoming involved. Parents need to become convinced that involvement will be an enjoyable experience, not a threatening and patronizing one. Make it a point to personally welcome all families; seek out those who seem to be withdrawn or uncomfortable. Learn all you can about parents, interests and abilities, and try to make those points of conversations. Actively seek opportunities for hesitant parents to use their experiences and skills to benefit your classroom and school. A true partnership is 50/50. Parents can and should be involved in the planning stages of a program, rather than coming aboard after everything has been decided for them. Listen and learn from what they have to say as well.

8. Parent Circumstances

Unfortunately, many families, as we know, have overwhelming circumstances. Many are living with housing, medical, and emotional issues, among others. You cannot solve their problems, but you may be able to provide needed information to families so that they can get on the road to solving their own problems. Look into providing advocacy or resources to help them secure the services they need to survive and flourish.

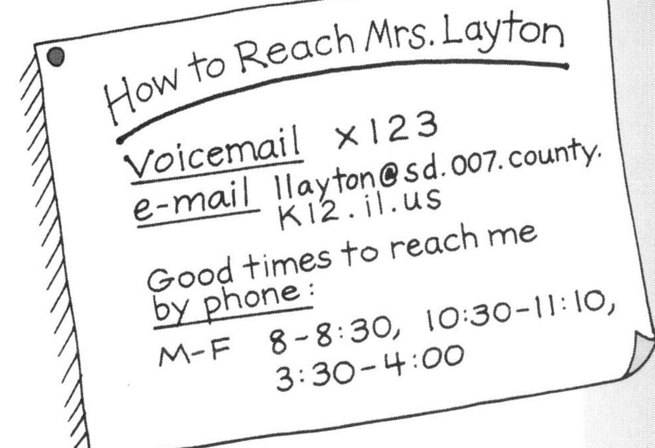

9. Busyness

Being busy is a reality for both teachers and parents, but it can function as a barrier to communication. When either side perceives the other to be so busy, they may not want to interrupt or appear bothersome. There are things that can be done to be perceived as more approachable. At the beginning of each day, make preparations for classroom activities before parents and children arrive. This will free you up to talk with parents as they drop off their children for the day. Arrange your classroom so that when parents enter, they have easy access to you. On your parent information board, let parents know the best times you can be reached that week. All of these seemingly small activities convey a message that you are there for parents. Ask parents for their schedules, and contact them during times when they are able to talk.

10. Money

Like time, money is another precious resource, especially in education. Fortunately, parent involvement does not cost a lot of money. True partnerships are built on relationships, not activities. Examine the activities that you plan and write out a budget. If you are unable to provide materials or supplies, ask for administrative or parent support.

Money for training is also an issue with partnership. Talk with your administrator and colleagues to see if training funds are available for discussion and study that would help parents and teachers work more successfully with families. Parent involvement affects every classroom, every teacher, and every child, yet few schools spend time talking about how to make it better. Working toward a partnership would be money and time well spent.

11. Differences and Beliefs

It is sometimes easier to criticize and complain about parents and what they do and do not do than to take time to understand and empathize. It is easy to attend selectively to information that is consistent with our own beliefs and conceptions. It is especially difficult when we may disagree or even disapprove of a family life-style or approach to parenting. These feelings may lead to barriers in forming relationships with these families as equals. Parents sense this and in turn avoid contact with teachers whose communication style and expectations are uncomfortably different from their own. It is important to be conscious that your behavior must reflect respect and understanding of all families despite real differences in background or beliefs. Be aware of both verbal and nonverbal messages that you send or that the families receive from you. Parents may receive those messages through a filter of many feelings, attitudes, and experiences. The greater number of small connections you make with individual families, the greater the chance a trusting relationship will occur.

Reaching Out

Many families can be labeled "hard to reach" because they are unable to attend school functions. Families can be hard to reach because they feel uncomfortable in school settings, they have problems getting to school because of transportation or child care issues, language and cultural issues offer communication challenges, or they may simply lack the confidence they need to communicate with you. We must remember that these families want to be involved and support their children, but for many of these reasons, they are having difficulty connecting.

Here are some suggestions to try with these families:

1. **Meet with families in a nonschool setting** (restaurant, community center, church).
2. **Try to connect by phone.** Start by sharing good news first.
3. **Ask a community member to be a liaison for you and the family.** A parent liaison can serve as an additional contact to help you respond to the needs and concerns of particular parents and families.
4. **Try multiple modes of communication** (letters, phone calls, home visits, etc.).
5. **Don't make assumptions.** All families have hopes and dreams for their children. Each family wants what they believe is best for their child.
6. **Ask and learn from families.** Understanding their perspective and situation is very important in opening lines of communication.
7. **If limited English proficiency presents a communication challenge, consider having letters, notes, and informational packets translated.** Have volunteers available to help you answer questions parents ask in their own language.
8. **Learn as much as you can about your students' community.** Culture, family, and the social structures and expectations regarding school will provide you with great insight into understanding and meeting the needs of all families in your classroom.

When it comes to partnerships with families, it all comes down to building relationships. Trust builds slowly over time. Remember, little things do mean a lot: It is the small, positive contacts that are most effective. Here are a few "little things" that can make a big difference in creating and building those bridges with parents in your classroom.

- Know each parent's name.
- Acknowledge parents by name.
- Make eye contact when saying hello.
- Shake hands with parents.
- Try to appear unhurried.
- Say something positive about the family's child.
- Talk to the child, if present; let him or her see your caring and connection to the children.
- Keep judgments to yourself.
- Be compassionate.
- Begin and end all conversations on a positive note.
- Recognize and respond to the positive contributions that parents make.
- *And smile!*

Where Do I Go from Here?

Successful partnerships are built upon the way we view families and the role they play in their child's development. Examining your attitudes and defining what parent involvement means to you personally will help you focus and attend to your goals. Do the activity at the right while keeping your classroom families in mind.

Three Things That *Families* Most Want from *Me*:

1. ______________________

2. ______________________

3. ______________________

Three Things That *I* Want Most from *Families*:

1. ______________________

2. ______________________

3. ______________________

Take a few moments to examine and think about the following questions.

- What do I see as my role in supporting parent involvement?
- What do I do in a typical day to involve families in the educational process?
- What would I like to be doing differently to involve families?
- What types of support from other staff would I need to do something different?

It is important to investigate your answers. They will become the goals and baseline for your work with families. Make sure that, from the very first time you meet families, you are building a foundation based on common goals and beliefs. This is a way that you can communicate what you need and expect from families, and they can do the same for you.

2 Communication

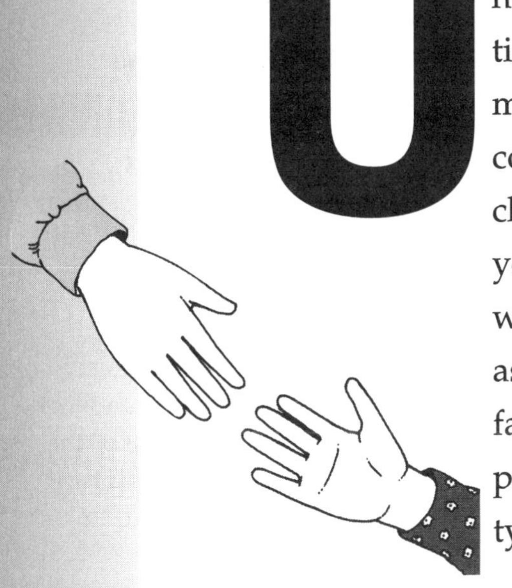

Understanding the importance for two-way communication with families is the first step to reaching out and making connections with parents; making time to communicate is your next challenge to greet. This chapter will serve as a tool to foster this process. Here you will find letters, handouts, and reminders to share with families. Use them as they are written or as guides as you seek to communicate more effectively with the families in your own classroom. Communication with parents and families can include any of the following types of information:

1. Information about special classroom activities
2. Descriptions of student activities
3. Information on school dates and events
4. Samples of children's work with descriptions of the types of activity and project in which they are engaged
5. Recipes or projects parents can do at home
6. Handouts with helpful hints for learning at home
7. Questionnaires to survey parents for their opinions
8. Updates and notes specifically pointing out positive student achievements and behaviors
9. Volunteer openings and updates

For communication to be powerful, it must be continuous, sustained, and reciprocal. It is important to have a balance of information sharing.

Following are ways in which teachers can learn the valuable information they need from parents and families.

1. Parent interest and volunteer surveys
2. Parent "report cards." Parents can and should periodically evaluate the school and have a venue to express concerns and interests
3. Personal interviews. These can be done at school, during a home visit, or at a common, agreed-upon location.
4. Group brainstorming sessions
5. Phone calls
6. Personal contact before and after school
7. Notes on student progress
8. Home visits

The following pages provide tools, such as sample letters for a parent handbook and items for a family information board, to facilitate parent communication. As you use these tools, feel free to be creative and make each work for you and your families. Try some of the following ideas, which are sure to capture parents' attention and even get them to "look twice!"

1. **Classroom Stationery.** Use the students' school pictures to create this one-of-a-kind stationery. Seeing their child's face on this special message is a guarantee to make them take note. *See the example on the next page.*
2. **Creative Language.** The way in which we position our words can be our most powerful tool. Just a few simple twists in your words send a powerful message to parents that their response and attendance is desired and necessary.
3. **Color and Shape.** Brightly colored paper is a definite standout in the book bag. Try cutting your note diagonally or in a unique shape. These subtle differences will make parents more aware of important events and messages.
4. **Student-made Items.** Anything that their child personalizes or creates is a definite hit.

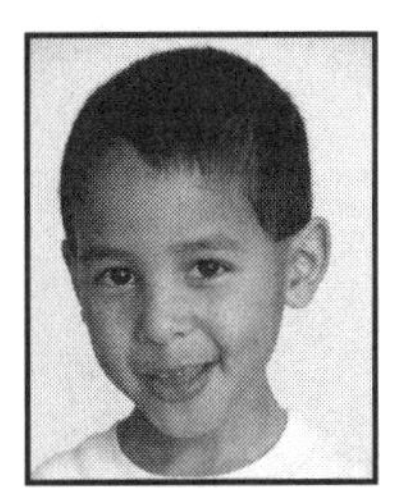
Jose

Tyreisha

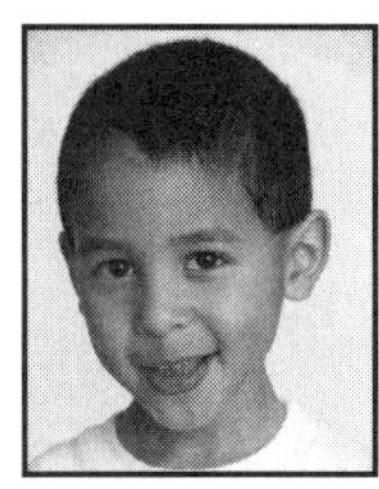
Robert

Sam

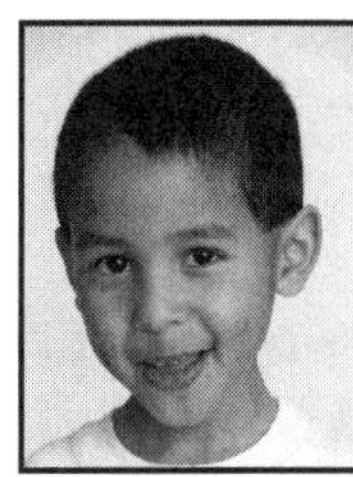
Tyrell

La Shay

Marcia

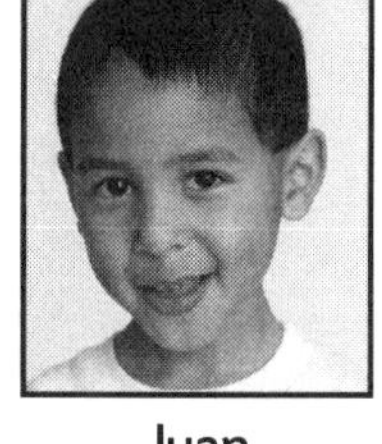
Juan

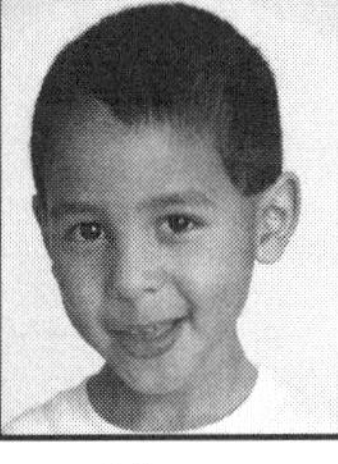
Hung

Alicia

Mia

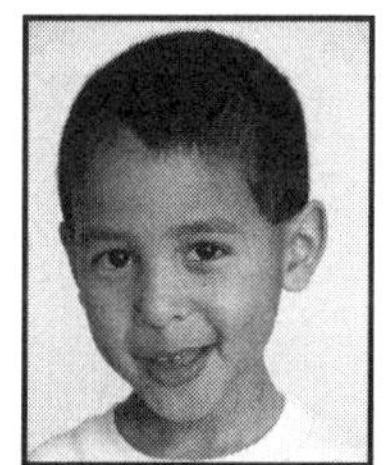
Chen

Jennifer

Abigail

Sample: **Classroom Stationery**

Stefon

Hannah

Katherine

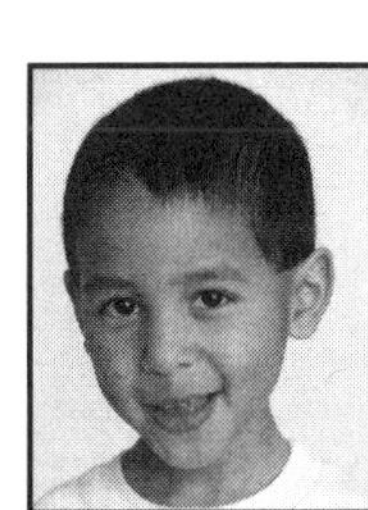
Ty

Charisse

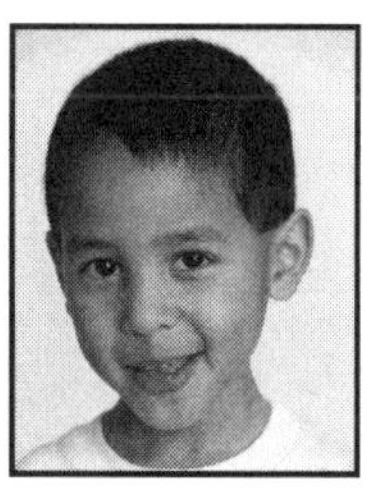
Joseph

Following are a few more ideas for communicating creatively with parents.

Sample Letters

First and foremost we must make our classrooms welcoming places where students and parents want to be. This can begin even before students walk through the classroom doors that first day. Try sending a welcoming letter to start off your year. Here are samples of letters that I use with students and parents.

Beginning-of-the-Year Letter to Students

Dear

My name is Mrs. Maiers, and I am going to be your first-grade teacher. Have you been doing lots of reading over the summer? Please bring your favorite story to class to share on the first day of school, and I will too!

I am very excited to meet you and your family. I love to read. I have been busy reading lots of good books. My room is Room 111. Look for me when you get to school that first day. I will be the one wearing the green dress! I can't wait to meet you—don't forget your favorite book!

I will see you next week!

Your teacher,
Mrs. Maiers

Beginning-of-the-Year Letter to Parents

Dear Parents,

The difference between a good school and an *outstanding* school is you! We know that when parents are involved, students do better. Relationships between parents and school improve, and everyone benefits.

You are the biggest influence in your child's life. What you believe is important, because your child will have the same beliefs. It is not just the quantity of time you spend at school, but the value that you place on education that makes the difference. It does not take a great deal of time to make a great difference in your child's education.

For you to be an advocate for your child, it is important that you know what is happening in our classroom and in your school. I will be sharing this information with you regularly, along with ways that we can support your child's growth and learning together.

Communication is the key to any successful relationship, so let's keep the lines open and active. I look forward to listening and learning from you, and I will share information back through newsletters, phone calls, and personal contacts with your family. Outside of our classroom, there will be a bulletin board containing the week's messages, upcoming events, and a place for you to share comments or concerns. There is an open-door policy in our room, so you can feel welcome anytime.

I look forward to a productive and exciting year of getting to know your child and family. If there is something that you would like to share with the class or me, I can be reached anytime before or after school. Here's to a great year together!

Sincerely,

Dear Families,

Our family reading night will be held on Wednesday evening. The students are very excited and eager for you to hear them read their new stories. They have been practicing! Please return the attached portion of this note as soon as possible. I look forward to seeing you all there!

- ☐ Yes, I will be attending.
  Name: ____________________
- ☐ A friend or family member will be coming in my place.
  Name: ____________________

Other Notes

I send other friendly notes throughout the year. Following are samples of other notes I've sent home to parents at various times. The first one makes two subtle statements:

1. Everyone is welcome. You are opening your classroom walls and including more than just mom or dad.
2. By not including a place for the parents to mark "no," this note expresses my interest that each family be represented at this very important function.

Volunteer SOS!

We are in need of parents to help with our upcoming family night. I have included a list of possible ways to assist. Please let me know if you are able to help out in any way. I appreciate all of your extra time and effort with this project. It would not be a success without you. The students are looking forward to this event.

Thank You,

Volunteering is something that you want to be ongoing, but creative reminders of special events throughout the year never hurt. To the left is a note that asks parents to help out at a special event.

Parent Handbook

You may choose to share with families important information organized in a handbook. A handbook prepared in time to be distributed during those first weeks of school serves to answer many questions and can be very helpful to parents and teachers. The handbook should be concise, attractive, and easy to read.

Sample handbook components:

- Philosophy of parent involvement for your school and classroom
- Arrival and departure times and places
- Calendar of important school events and meetings
- List of needed supplies
- Phone numbers
- Program and staff descriptions
- Classroom procedures (parties, birthdays, holidays)
- Topics and themes
- Homework and discipline policy
- Request for volunteer assistance
- Policy for late arrival, early departure, and emergencies
- Tips to nurture development

Family Information Board

There should be a designated place where parents can receive updated information about your classroom events and activities. This place should be in or near your classroom. You may not have an opportunity to connect with them face-to-face every day, and notes may get lost. This centrally located information center will be a constant source of events, news, reciprocal communication, and more. You can make this as simple or creative as you wish.

Here are some suggestions of possible items you may want to include:

- Upcoming school events (date, time, location)
- Classroom calendar
- Requests for parent assistance
- Displays of student artwork or writing
- Lunch menu
- Relevant community news
- Newspaper articles, clippings, or editorials of interest
- Copies of the classroom newsletter
- Before- and after-school program schedules
- Upcoming events
- Parent-to-teacher or parent-to-parent messages
- Blank areas for parents to share comments and suggestions

The "Fridge"

The refrigerator is often the central location in each household; it displays some of a family's most prized possessions. It is not only a place to store food and beverages, but it often serves as the hub of communication. Pinned, taped, and held by magnets are the mementos of special people and events that keep each family on track. Household chores, work and play schedules, and prized photo moments are displayed and used.

Here is a way to uniquely recreate that familiar and safe communication tool in your classroom. It will not only serve as a great conversation piece, but it will remind families of the meaningful uses of reading and writing that they do every day in their own homes. This can be used in place of or in addition to your current parent information area.

Materials:

1 large piece of cardboard *(the side of a stove or appliance box works well)*

Aluminum foil *(several feet, depending on the size of the model)*

White or cream tempera paint

Alphabet letter cutouts

Construction paper

Markers

Instructions:

1. Cut the cardboard in two large rectangular shapes. The top piece should be about one-third the size of the bottom.
2. Cover the cardboard shapes with foil. Wrap several pieces of the foil in a long shape to create the door handle.
3. Paint over the foil with white or cream paint to give your refrigerator door a more "authentic" metal look.
4. Use construction paper and markers to create refrigerator magnets. These magnets can be placed to hold up notes and messages to the parents about upcoming classroom and school events. The magnets can be glued directly to the display.
5. Use the cutout letters to create highlighted areas to draw parents' attention to events that need their attention. *For example:*
   School calendar
   Supplies
   Student of the Week
   Weekly news
6. Place your classroom "refrigerator" on your classroom door or on a wall next to or near your classroom. Encourage parents to read and use this tool of communication just as they would at home. Leave an open space for parent comments and input.

Sample Parent Questionnaire or Interview

The kinds of questions we ask families guide us in our understanding of parents' thoughts, feelings, and values. It is likely that each student in your classroom represents a different social, ethnic, financial, or educational background. Often, in our questions about how much parents read each night to their child or when families visit the library, we miss valuable opportunities to learn all that we can from families. As we gain this valuable information through our conversations, we gain a better sense of who the children are and can expand our ability to meet their needs in our diverse classrooms and society.

We must value what every family does to support their child's literacy learning and development. The following can be used as possible questions you may want to use with your families. All the questions are not intended to be used at one time, and some you will want to ask as the year progresses and families feel more comfortable and open to sharing.

As you ask these questions, seek to learn from each answer. The more you understand each family, the better you can help your students.

Possible questions to ask:

What is your child's most special attribute?

What does you child enjoy doing when he or she is not at school?

How does your family spend its free time?

What is the most rewarding part about being a parent?

What is the hardest part about being a parent?

What is the most effective way to help your child when a problem arises?

Does your child see himself or herself as a successful reader and writer? How do you know?

What was your most successful school experience?

What was your most challenging school experience?

What method of discipline reaches your child most effectively?

What does your home schedule look like?

What family routines do you follow?

What is the most enjoyable activity that you and your child do together?

Tell me about your child growing up.

Are there any problems of which I should be aware that would affect your child's learning?

What type of summer activities does your child enjoy?

Does your family have opportunities to visit the library? Do you have library cards?

What is your child's dream for when he or she grows up?

What are your hopes for your child as he or she grows up?

Who are the important people in your child's life?

What has your child watched you do or learned from you of which you are really proud?

Let these questions serve as a beginning point for creating those important connections. Share the list with colleagues, add to it, adapt, and modify it as you see fit. Think about the kinds of information that will help you respond, respect, and understand families more deeply. The value we place on all parents' knowledge will help us use that knowledge for constructive purposes.

The Positive Phone Call

Imagine the impact when parents receive a phone call from you just to say how much their child has progressed or how excited you were to have their child in your classroom. The response is quite amazing! This communication technique is one of the most powerful ways you can use to connect with families. Teachers often use the telephone to contact parents in case of emergency or if a problem occurs. When a telephone call from school carries information that is positive, the atmosphere between the home and school is greatly improved.

Planning these calls is an important part of continued success. Before calling a parent, gather the following information about the family:

Date of call: ______________________

Time: ______________________

Student: ______________________

Telephone number: ______________________

Best time to reach parents: ______________________

Use the following "script" for each call:

1. Introduce yourself (if this is your first welcoming call).
2. State the purpose of the call.
3. Share a specific, positive comment about the student (behavior, academic improvement, positive attitude).
4. Allow time for parent comments.
5. Speak to the student (optional; your goal is parent connection and communication).
6. On the following contact sheet, document and date the call.
7. On the contact sheet, jot down thoughts or comments on the phone call.

Positive Phone Call Contact Record

Student Name: ______________________ Date: ____________

Positive Behavior Documented: ______________________

____

Parent's Comments: ______________________

____

Notes: ______________________

____

Student Name: ______________________ Date: ____________

Positive Behavior Documented: ______________________

____

Parent's Comments: ______________________

____

Notes: ______________________

____

Student Name: ______________________ Date: ____________

Positive Behavior Documented: ______________________

____

Parent's Comments: ______________________

____

Notes: ______________________

____

Student Name: ______________________ Date: ____________

Positive Behavior Documented: ______________________

____

Parent's Comments: ______________________

____

Notes: ______________________

____

Asking Parents to Volunteer

A great way to involve parents in your classroom is to invite them to volunteer. You get needed help while they see what happens in the class on a day-to-day basis. The first step in this process is to ask parents about their availability and their special interests or hobbies. On the following pages are two letters that you can send as is or use as guides for your own invitations to volunteer.

Once you have received parents' responses, record each family's information on the Family Volunteer Information form (see p. 35). This will give you an easy-to-access archive of your volunteers' interests and availability.

Once parents are in your classroom, helping out on a regular basis, use the following list of simple reminders to make this a smooth, successful experience for everyone involved.

1. Don't be reluctant to involve parents in many parts of your school program. The more they participate, the easier it is for you and them, and of course, the better for the children.
2. Begin gradually by finding one or two instructional, assisting, supervisory, or housekeeping opportunities for each volunteer. Don't overwhelm a parent with too many tasks at once. Increase the responsibilities as he or she becomes more confident.
3. If volunteers are tutoring small groups, remember to give opportunities to work at a variety of learning levels.
4. Be sure to set aside time to talk with that parent volunteer about what he or she has done. Get feedback about the children with whom he or she has worked.
5. Plan ahead for your parent volunteers, especially at the early stages. Be sure you communicate your plans and direction explicitly.
6. Encourage volunteers to come in on a regular schedule. The effectiveness of volunteers is minimized if you cannot plan for them on a regular basis.
7. Discuss your program and the reasons for your activities. Parent volunteers often become the most outspoken advocates for your child's education.
8. Use the individual strengths of each parent.
9. Encourage parents to view their own child objectively as a member of the total classroom. It may be a new experience for a child to have his or her mother or father in the classroom, and it may take time for everyone to adjust to this new situation.
10. Volunteers don't have to be parents only. Grandpas, grandmas, aunts, uncles, and members of the community may be eager and ready. They may just be waiting for an invitation from you.
11. Remember to give support, encouragement, and praise. Your small gestures will make parents and volunteers happy and coming back.
12. Ask parents to leave behind what they see of any child's behavior in the classroom. Every child eventually has a bad day, and stories of that bad day should not follow the child throughout the school year.

We Need You!

Dear Families,

You are an important part of our school and classroom community. You are a wealth of knowledge and talent that would make wonderful additions to your child's learning and education. Please take a few moments to fill out the following information so that we can work together to create the best program possible for your child. I understand that schedules are busy, and I appreciate your time. Remember that you can help in many ways. Coming to our classroom is just one option. Thank you again, and I look forward to sharing our talents.

Sincerely,

Child's Name ______________________________

Parent's Name ______________________________

Please mark any of the following activities with which you would be interested in helping. Mark as many as you like.

- ☐ Helping during the school day
- ☐ Helping out in your child's classroom
- ☐ Field trips
- ☐ Bulletin boards
- ☐ Reading stories to students
- ☐ Helping children at learning centers
- ☐ Preparing learning materials
- ☐ Computer lab monitor
- ☐ Listening to students read
- ☐ Special celebration preparation
- ☐ Laminating and cutting out
- ☐ Sharing a special talent (painting, cooking, dance, music)
- ☐ Speaking at school about your job

We Need You!

Dear Families,

You are your child's first and most important teacher. We are always looking to add new life to our classroom learning. If you have a special hobby or talent, we would love to have you share those with us. Below are some of the things we will be studying this semester.

(Insert your own school theme or classroom subject.)

Plants and Gardening
Transportation
Space and Astronomy
State History

Talent Search Wish List:
Can You, Would You . . .

- ☐ Cook a special recipe
- ☐ Sew, knit, or crochet
- ☐ Teach us a game
- ☐ Read a special story to us
- ☐ Help us at learning centers
- ☐ Share a family tradition
- ☐ Share a piece of your history or family heritage
- ☐ Color or assist with assembling learning materials at home
- ☐ Talk with us about your job or career
- ☐ Show us a special collection (coins, stamps, books)

Other ideas to share ______________________________

____

Sincerely,

Family Volunteer Information

Child's Name: ______ Parent's Name: ______
Father: Home Phone: ______ Work Phone: ______
Mother: Home Phone: ______ Work Phone: ______
Type of Involvement Preferred: During School Options: ______
At Home Options: ______
Other: ______
Additional Family Information: ______

Child's Name: ______ Parent's Name: ______
Father: Home Phone: ______ Work Phone: ______
Mother: Home Phone: ______ Work Phone: ______
Type of Involvement Preferred: During School Options: ______
At Home Options: ______
Other: ______
Additional Family Information: ______

Child's Name: ______ Parent's Name: ______
Father: Home Phone: ______ Work Phone: ______
Mother: Home Phone: ______ Work Phone: ______
Type of Involvement Preferred: During School Options: ______
At Home Options: ______
Other: ______
Additional Family Information: ______

Child's Name: ______ Parent's Name: ______
Father: Home Phone: ______ Work Phone: ______
Mother: Home Phone: ______ Work Phone: ______
Type of Involvement Preferred: During School Options: ______
At Home Options: ______
Other: ______
Additional Family Information: ______

Home Visits

Home visits can be a wonderful experience for students, parents, and teachers. Call parents at the beginning of the school year and schedule a convenient time that you can meet with the students and the family on their "home turf." Parents feel more welcomed and relaxed in familiar surroundings, and students see home and school as a team working together. It offers you a better perspective on the student's life away from the school grounds.

Home visits can show the parents that you are willing to "go the extra mile" to involve all parents in their child's education. Home visits help you demonstrate your interest in students' families and understand your students better by seeing their home environments. Teachers who have made home visits say they build stronger relationships with families much more quickly and parents and children respond positively to their extra effort.

Following are tips for successful home visits:

1. Schedule visits during times that are convenient for families. You may want to send a note or give parents a phone call to find times that work out for both of you. Call ahead for convenient times.
2. Plan to make the first visit a positive one. Do not base the first visit on a problematic situation.
3. Let the students know how excited you are to be talking with them at home.
4. Home visits done early, even before the school year starts, can set a really positive tone. It is a way for you to build stronger relationships with parents and their children before a problem may arise.
5. Plan for the visit. Have a simple agenda, and come prepared.
6. Document your visit with parents by making notes about important information that was shared during the visit. This information will help open and continue communication throughout the school year.
7. Don't overwhelm parents by asking them to fill out forms of information. Gathering information is important, but it must not seem like an interrogation to families.

Use the following pages as tools to help in scheduling and organizing the information gained from this valuable time with parents.

Schedule for Home Visits

Student	Parent	Family Address	Phone Number	Date of Visit	Time Visited
1.					
2.					
3.					
4.					
5.					
6.					
7.					
8.					
9.					
10.					
11.					
12.					
13.					
14.					
15.					
16.					
17.					
18.					
22.					
23.					
24.					
25.					
26.					
27.					
28.					
29.					
30.					

Sample Parent Letter for Home Visit

Dear_________________,

Thank you for allowing me to visit your child and family. I look forward to meeting you. It is important for me to learn as much from you as your child may from me. If you would take a few moments before I come to share some of this valuable information with me, it would be greatly appreciated.

- When would be the best time to visit?
- Please share what makes you most excited about the coming school year.
- Do you have any questions or concerns?
- What do you and your child enjoy doing together outside of school?
- What is your child's favorite hobby or area of interest?
- Are they any problems that you feel I should be aware of?
- Tell me something special about your child.

Thank you for your time. I will contact you soon to schedule this visit.

Sincerely,

Sample Home Visit Data Collection Form

Student Name: Date Visited:

Parent/Guardian Name:

Sibling Names and Ages:

Mother's Information: Age: Occupation:

Special Interest/Hobbies:

Phone Number: Home: Work:

Father's Information: Age: Occupation:

Special Interest/Hobbies:

Phone Number: Home: Work:

Times Best Reached:

Home Visit Reflection/Comments:

Communicating All Year Long: *Setting Up a Parent Resource Center*

Parent resource centers can be invaluable for offering a place throughout the year for parents to feel welcome and for fostering ongoing communication. In these ways, parent resource centers can support parents as both teachers and learners. The centers do not have to be elaborate to be effective and can range from an entire room in the school that serves all families to a table in your classroom for your students' families. The goal is to send the message to parents that they belong and are a welcomed resource to the school.

A resource center can provide space and materials where parents can get together with other parents and school staff to learn how to assist children at home. Parents come to such a center for educational materials, books, training, or meetings.

Following is list of items that you may use to support parents:

- Reading materials for students, as well as books on parenting
- Educational games and materials for parents to play with their child
- Toys and books for students to use as their parents visit the center
- Video and audio tapes available to check out for home use
- Pamphlets on topics that interest families, ranging from tips on reading aloud to assisting with discipline issues. These are usually very inexpensive and available from professional organizations and community centers.
- Information about school and community events
- A suggestion box for parents to share thoughts, feelings, and questions about the school
- Comfortable furniture, where parents can sit as they use the resources or talk with other parents visiting the center

Use your imagination to brainstorm possible ways to use or stock the resource center. As the resource center grows, you may ask parents to volunteer or provide help to other parents visiting the resource area. ■

3 Letters to Parents

Sharing Balanced Literacy Practices with Families

School has dramatically changed since many parents were there. Schools are responding to this new literacy demand in unique and strategic ways. The effort to meet society's increasingly higher literacy demands and to provide the highest quality educational practice has been confusing and even overwhelming for us. As we learn more about how children learn, and how best to teach them, we have multiple opportunities to discuss these changes with other teachers and districts and staffs across the nation.

Parents, on the other hand, have not had the privilege to be inserviced and trained on the latest techniques and teaching practice. When they walk into our classrooms and help their children with information sent home, they may be seeing and feeling something quite different from what they know or have experienced. In the spirit of Frank Smith and the work he has done to let children be a part of the "literacy club," we too must afford the same for their families.

If our goal is to promote and strengthen involvement, parents need to be aware and informed of the most current practice and programs we are implementing in our classrooms. Many learning strategies students experience every day, such as guided reading and literature circles, may be unfamiliar terms to their parents. We cannot expect their educational nurture and support at home if they do not understand what these practices are and how they can extend the learning at home. It is important that they understand both the how and why of our instruction. Parents need to be "re-introduced" to our classrooms. To elicit their support, it is our job to keep them updated and informed about the different methods, theories, and philosophies in their child's learning environment. The following letters will help you do just that. Send them as is, or use them as a basis for writing your own.

Teacher Adaptations to Letter on Page 41:

You may want to specify a time for these balanced reading and writing activities and invite parents to observe and participate. Remember: If we want their support and encouragement at home, we must inform them of what we are doing at school!

Sample Letter **Introducing Balanced Literacy to Parents**

Dear Families,

As you visit our classroom throughout the year, you will be seeing your child engaged in many different reading and writing experiences. It is important that you know how and understand what your child is doing at school so we can best support one another. Each week I will be sending you a letter describing one of the many reading and writing activities your child participates in during a day in our classroom. When your child comes home and describes what he or she has been doing in class, you will have a better idea of what he or she is talking about. If you have any questions, please don't hesitate to call. I look forward to your visit.

Sincerely,

Reading Aloud at Home

Dear Families,

When you visit our classroom or hear your child talk about stories we have shared together, you will learn that I read out loud to the students every day. It is a deliberate part of my reading program, not something we do just on special occasions. Children benefit a great deal from having books read out loud to them each day.

Reading aloud helps children learn:

1. First and foremost, the pure pleasure and joy of reading. They learn to discover why it is important to learn to read.
2. What books sound like. The language of books is very different than a spoken language. I need to expose the students to many different types of books before they are ready to begin reading and writing them on their own.
3. How good reading sounds. I provide children with a model for reading with excitement and emotion. I read in my "best reading voice" so they hear a flowing, fluent story told.
4. What good books have to share. Books are for both pleasure and knowledge. After each story, we talk about how we all reacted to the book, and what we learned as well. Great literature opens up new worlds of learning in my classroom!

Here's what you can do to support this practice at home:

- Continue to read aloud to them each night. There are never too many books to hear. Fifteen minutes is all you need.
- Make the event an enjoyable time for you and your child. You may even want to set aside a special time and place.
- Read as many different types and kinds of books as you can; picture books, nonfiction, poems, etc.
- Remember that talk about the book is what makes the time special. Ask lots of questions, and let your child do the same.

Happy reading at home!

Sincerely,

The ABCs of Listening to My Child Read

Always be positive. This should be an enjoyable, stress-free time.

Be patient. Sometimes your child will stumble. Pause for a moment and let him or her work through the problem with your support. Praise all of his or her efforts, and keep an encouraging tone.

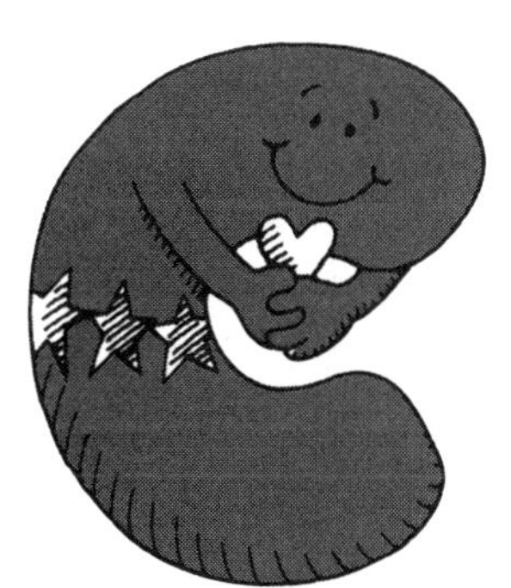

Cherish this special time. Your child will remember it for years!

Shared Reading

Dear Families,

You may come into the classroom and see all the students sitting with me gathered on the carpet around a "Big Book" or "Poster Book." This is a very large book, large enough for the whole class to see pictures and read the text together, just as you would do at home with your favorite bedtime story. This is a time called "Shared Reading." In Shared Reading, we may revisit and reread a book many times, but the children are actively involved in each new reading. I often pause in the reading and ask the children to predict what will happen next. Many of the books I choose include predictable text so that the children can easily chime in with a word or predictable phrase. Over the many times we read the books, students become familiar with the words and formats and begin to recognize and feel confident as they read on their own. I can model what I expect of them as readers when they go to work on their own books. Just as children learn to walk and talk at different times and rates, the same holds true for reading and writing. During Shared Reading, I can support each student in my classroom as he or she works through the reading process as individuals.

Shared Reading helps children learn that:

- Books are fun and carry a message; enjoyment is first and foremost.
- The print carries a message.
- Direction is important to reading; readers read from top to bottom and left to right.
- There is an exact match between the spoken language and written word.

You may see me or hear the children talk about such activities as using a special pointer, frame, or tape to illustrate these concepts and practice word identification skills.

Here is what you can do to support this practice at home:

- Encourage all of your child's efforts; one of the primary purposes of shared reading is to support your child's reading successes.
- Choose books that have repetitive phrases and language patterns so that your child can "chime" in whenever able. Your child may memorize portions of the book. This is an important step in the reading process and should be praised as well.
- Have your child trace the print as you read. You may even have him or her "frame" words or letters with fingers.
- When your child shows an interest in print, run your fingers lightly under the words as you read. This will highlight both the direction a reader reads and the relationship between the print and story.

Sincerely,

Guided Reading

Dear Families,

You may hear your child talk about or share the newest book he or she read during reading group time. There is a time in our day that I meet in small groups with students to read books that I pick specifically to help them grow in their reading process. This "Guided Reading" is the heart of our reading program.

This group may be different than the ones you remember or may have participated in during your elementary years. You may recall only getting to read one page or passage at a time or learning specific vocabulary words for that story. During Guided Reading, every child in the classroom is not reading the same story. Each group of five or six children has a book meant for that group's reading level, so that they are able to read progressively more challenging text on their own. Our goal in Guided Reading is for your child to gain control over the reading process by exposure to books that are supportive enough to keep him or her reading, but contain enough challenge to make your child "work" through the book using his or her own reading strategies. It is important to keep each group small so I can carefully watch this happen and move each child onto more challenging books when he or she is ready.

Guided Reading helps children learn:

- To celebrate all reading tries and accomplishments. Each book your child works through in our group is a triumph.
- To become aware of their own thinking and how they work out their own reading problems.
- To become fluent, independent, and confident readers.

Here is what you can do to support this practice at home:

- Celebrate! Have your child read new books to you at home.
- Compliment the things you see that good readers do (see attached list).
- Encourage silent reading. Practice makes perfect!

Sincerely,

What Do Good Readers Do?

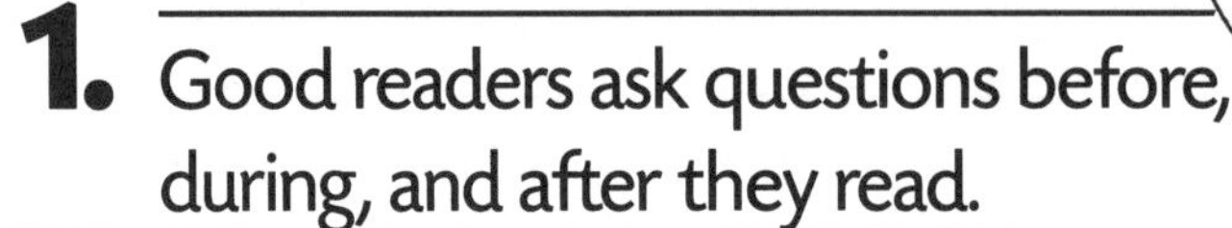

1. Good readers ask questions before, during, and after they read.
2. Good readers go back and reread for understanding.
3. Good readers use what they know to make predictions.
4. Good readers know when they make a mistake and go back to fix it.
5. Good readers use many different ways to work out a word that they don't recognize.
6. Good readers read fluently with expression.
7. Good readers use their background and experience to help them understand the book.
8. Good readers make connections to other books they have read.
9. Good readers understand what they have read and can talk about those understandings.
10. Good readers **READ, READ, READ!**

Silent Reading

Dear Families,

Every day in our classroom, we stop and get our favorite books, find a cozy spot in the room, and read away! This is what we call D.E.A.R. (Drop Everything And Read). Both the students and I read. If you were to visit during D.E.A.R. time, you would be able to hear a pin drop on our classroom floor. The students are so excited about this time, which we call "Silent Reading," when they read their favorites and take time to enjoy reading. The time we set aside for Silent Reading is important for several reasons.

Silent Reading helps children learn:

- To carefully select reading materials that help them become confident, fluent readers.
- That reading is very important, so vital that nothing interferes with our silent reading time; it is a special time during our day.
- To practice all the skills and strategies that we have worked on in small and whole-group time on their own.

Here is what you can do to support this practice at home:

- Set aside time each day for your child to read for an uninterrupted time frame (5 to 15 minutes).
- Talk with your child about what kinds of books he or she selects to read; this will help you learn about his or her goals and interests.
- Keep a special place in the house to store books for your child. This can be a shelf or box that your child can claim as his or her own.
- Model silent reading yourself. Let your child see you reading for pleasure. You may even choose to do this reading at the same time and have D.E.A.R. time as a family each evening.

Sincerely,

The BIG Black Hole

Language Experience

Dear Families,

Both spoken and written language play an important role in your child's literacy development. Your child's oral language is the foundation for all of his or her written language development. It is important for us to validate what children learn through language and understand what their talk represents. During a portion of our day that I call "Language Experience," the children are given opportunities to express their thoughts and understandings of new learning that has occurred. During a shared experience, such as a story I have read aloud, a field trip, or experiment, students will be invited to respond to the experience in some way. I will use that common experience and record our thoughts and understandings on a chart or the chalkboard. I will make a point to connect their oral language to a written form. They will see their own thoughts and words validated and written down. We will use this as a point of discussion or extension of the experience.

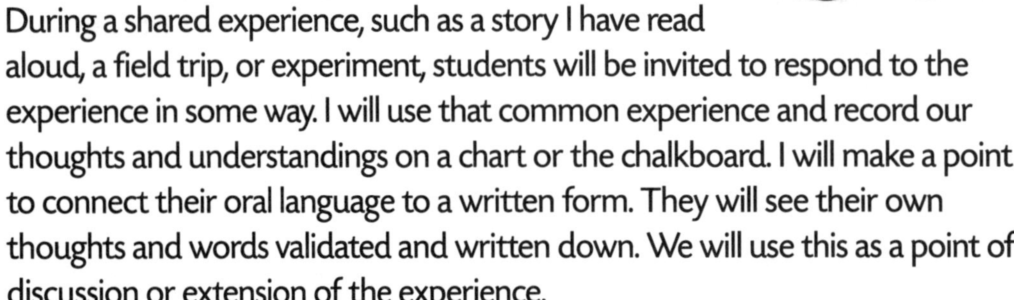

Language Experience helps children learn that:

- Their ideas are valued and respected.
- Written language serves many purposes.
- Talking helps them write.
- Writing can be a collaborative process.

Here is what you can do to support this practice at home:

- Encourage your child to talk about his/her learning.
- Have your child describe objects, people, and events. Record your child's thoughts as he or she is talking about the learning.
- Facilitate elaboration and explanation. As your child expresses ideas, affirm and value how he or she is thinking.

Sincerely,

Independent Writing

Dear Families,

Just as we set aside time every day in our classroom for students to read and enjoy books silently, we place that same value for time set aside for students to express themselves in writing. It is important that there is time each day to practice and explore all the different ways that they can record their thoughts and feelings in a written format. Children should write for many reasons and purposes, so we practice writing lists, responding to books we have read, sharing personal notes with one another, and sharing our thoughts in a personal journal. Writing needs to be a lifelong skill, and this time set aside in our day for Independent Writing lets them celebrate and experience the joy of being a writer.

Independent Writing helps children learn:

- To share their thoughts and ideas in written form.
- That writing can be fun and rewarding.
- That good writing continues over time.
- That writers write for many reasons and have different purposes for their writing.

Here is what you can do to support this practice at home:

- Provide uninterrupted time to let your child explore the writing process.
- Set up an area with "writer's tools." (See the attached list of suggested items for a writer's toolbox.)
- Encourage your child to share his or her ideas with you. This is not a time for corrections. Responding as a reader to what your child has written will be most important.

Sincerely,

The Writer's Toolbox

Suggested Supplies Every Writer Can Use

Some children like having a special place where they have all the materials they need so they can write; others like writing here and there as they feel the need. All children like having a wonderful supply of materials handy when the moment arrives. Here are a few suggested supplies.

1. A variety of good books for ideas and as models
2. Paper of all types (scraps, notebook, colored, pictured)
3. Post cards, old greeting cards, and blank forms or paper for quick notes
4. Pencils, markers, colored pencils, and crayons
5. Stapler and staples
6. Writing resources (dictionary, thesaurus, encyclopedia)
7. A personal dictionary to store their own important words (This can be any kind of notebook.)
8. A place to store pieces still in progress (This can be a small box or drawer. It is important to have a place where all supplies and work can be organized.)
9. Envelopes, any type or size (Stickers work great for stamps.)
10. A computer, if one is available (For many students, this is very motivating and is often more efficient than traditional pencil-and-paper writing.)

Literature Circles

Dear Families,

Along with our guided reading groups, your child will be participating in another reading time that we call "Literature Circles." This is an exciting time for our class, because we come together and talk about our favorite authors and the stories they write. Our Literature Circle time is very similar to what grown-ups would be doing in a book club. We meet regularly to talk about books the children have chosen to read for pleasure. The students may all be reading the same book and discussing many aspects of the story, or we may choose to read different books by the same author and compare and contrast the books. This is a time to which we all look forward and extends what we do in guided reading. Students must be able to fully understand and comprehend the book they have read in order to engage in meaningful conversation over the story.

Literature Circles help children learn:

- That readers react and respond to books by sharing their thoughts and feelings with other readers.
- That readers can have different opinions and feelings over the same book. Students learn to respect and respond to thoughts and comments from other group members.
- To gain deeper and more complex meanings from the texts that they read. Each time we reread a book and talk about how that book may be like others we have read or how the story made us feel, the students gain a deeper level of understanding of the meaning in that book.

Here is what you can do to support this practice at home:

- Ask your child to share the book he or she is working on for literature discussion group.
- Encourage your child to respond in different ways to literature (art, writing, or drama).
- Ask your child about his or her reactions, feelings, and questions about the story he or she is reading.
- Encourage your child to think about the author's reason for writing the story, how the story makes him or her feel, and if he or she can think of other stories or experiences that relate to this book.

Sincerely,

Writer's Workshop

Dear Families,

Our classroom guided writing time is called "Writer's Workshop." It is a way for me to help the children learn to write as they construct individual pieces of writing. I provide students with guidance, assistance, and feedback. During short, focused writing lessons, I help students with everything from selecting a topic to learning punctuation. The topics I choose emerge from what I see in their writing as well as skills that I feel the students will need to be successful writers. I hold these conferences for the whole class and small groups of children. I also meet with students individually on writing pieces. We hold our workshop each day. It is important that the students know they have time built in for this teacher-facilitated writing time. Children take their writing through successive stages, including:

1. **Creating and writing a draft,** a first-time piece of writing that can be shared with others for constructive feedback and comments.
2. **Revising and editing that draft.** This is the time for students to revise, edit, and thereby improve their writing skills.
3. **Publishing the work.** Work is published when a child is ready to put it in a form that others can see.

We want our students to write as real writers in the real world do—to rehearse, draft, revise, edit, proofread, and share. We practice writing daily for a variety of purposes and a wide range of audiences. It is important that students take responsibility for and take control of their own writing processes.

Writer's Workshop helps children learn:

- To develop their writing voice.
- To build their abilities to write different words and use punctuation and grammar.
- To recognize that writing has succeeded in its purpose when it has been read and understood by the intended audience.
- To monitor and improve the quality of their own writing and spend time working to become an independent writer who enjoys writing.

Here is what you can do to support this practice at home:

- Provide help if your child asks for it. Talk over ideas to clarify thinking. Read the draft and comment first on the things you like.
- Help with spelling, grammar, and punctuation, if you are asked.
- Try to be a friend rather than a writing critic. Leave the final decisions in the hands of the writer. This will encourage independence.
- Praise constantly. Any piece of writing has room for improvement, but it is important that you point out the good aspects and efforts that went into producing it.
- Demonstrate the value of your child's writing by finding a prominent place around the house to display it.

Sincerely,

4 Letters to Parents

Letting Them Know How They Can Help at Home

Parents want to help support their child's literacy development but often do not know specific activities to do at home. The following letters contain activities and ideas for parents who want to help their children at home. There is a wide range and variety of activities, so families will have many choices. You may choose to send the letters as they are or create your own versions. Stress to parents that there is no one way to do these activities. Encourage them to make changes to suit their child's and family's needs. These activities are designed to build attitudes and behaviors that students will need to be successful in school and life.

Helping Your Child with Words and Letters

Dear Families,

Helping your child read is one of the most exciting things parents do. Part of the reading process is learning words and letters. Here are some ideas to try when you are reading and writing with your child.

1. Reading to your child every day not only teaches them the joy of reading but also teaches that ideas can be written down, and the marks on the paper stand for the words we use and the sounds we make.

2. Make a name plate spelling out your child's first name with large black letters. Cut apart each letter and place it in a plastic bag or envelope. This can become a name puzzle that your child can use for practice each day. When he or she has learned all the letters in his or her name, you can add last name, middle name, names of family members, and so on.

3. Celebrate and keep a record of the new words your child learns. Have your child keep each learned word in a personal journal or dictionary or on index cards. Keep the cards handy, and use them later for reinforcement and practice. Your child will feel a sense of accomplishment and ownership as he or she keeps adding to the ever-growing list of knowledge.

Happy reading and learning!

Sincerely,

Learning Letters Can Be Fun!

Dear Families,

Here are some new ways to make learning letters even more fun.

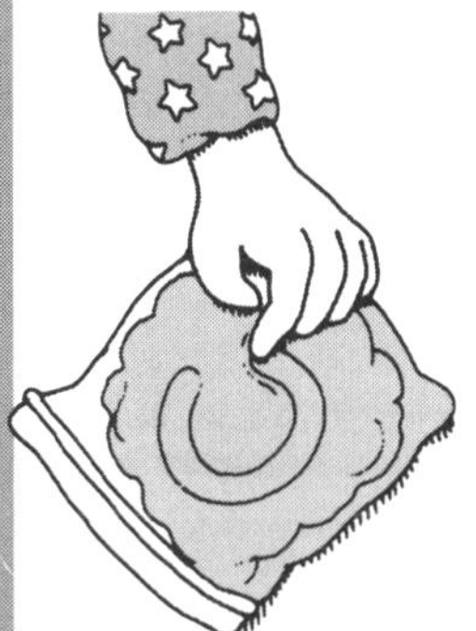

Gooey Letter Bags

You will need:

1/2 cup of hair gel

Food coloring

Locking sandwich bag

Place the hair gel and two drops of food coloring in the bag and mix until blended. Make sure the bag is tightly closed. Have your child practice the alphabet by forming letters in the gel. Children love this!

Letters in the Sand

You will need:

1/2 cup fine sand (local hardware store)

Small, shallow, rectangular tray

Place the sand in the tray, and have your child make the letters in the sand. They love the feel of the cool, soft sand between their fingers.

Eating the Alphabet

You will need:

2 packages of refrigerator biscuit dough

Role out the biscuits with your child, and form the letters in his or her name. Bake 15 minutes, and eat your way through the letters!

Have fun!

Sincerely,

I Am an Artist

Dear Families,

Having your child express himself or herself through art is a very powerful learning tool. Here are some unique painting activities to try at home.

Soap Paint

1 cup laundry soap flakes

$1\frac{1}{4}$ cup water

$\frac{1}{3}$ cup liquid starch

Mix together. Beat with a whisk for 3 minutes.

Gelatin Paint

Any flavor of gelatin

Boiling water *(enough to make the gelatin the consistency of finger paint)*

Mix ingredients together, and try this on glossy paper. Kids love the smell and feel of the paint.

Sand Paint

Tempera paint (powder)

Sand

Mix the dry tempera paint with the sand. Let your child spread glue on the picture, and then sprinkle on sand.

Puffed-up Paint

Flour

Salt

Water

Tempera paint

Mix equal amounts of flour, salt, and water. Add liquid tempera paint for the color. Pour mix into squeeze bottles and begin painting. (Mixture will harden into a puffy shape.)

Your child can paint a picture in response to a book you've read together, create a new page or pages for a story using the same pattern, or paint the words and letters they know. Let your imaginations run wild!

Happy painting!

Sincerely,

Helping Your Child Through a Book

Dear Families,

We hate to see children struggle, and it is our first instinct to jump in and "save" them from frustration. To help your child grow into an independent reader, it is important that the books he or she chooses to read have some element of challenge. Here are some prompts to help you avoid intervening when you and your child read together. These statements will prompt your child to figure out the right strategy. Your words will help nudge him or her in the right direction.

When your child gets off-track, you could say:

"Try pointing to the words as you read."
"Use your finger to help you keep track."
"Try it again and touch the words as your mouth says them."

When your child substitutes an incorrect word:

"Would that make sense? Try that again."
"What would sound right?"
"Is that the word? Why or why not?"

When your child stops at an unknown word:

"Look at the picture—does it help?"
"Read it again, what would make sense?"
"Is there any part or chunk of the word you can read?"

When your child makes an attempt to correct a mistake:

"Great job. You knew something wasn't right!"
"Great thinking. Good readers fix their mistakes!"
"You figured that out yourself."
"You got it. Let's try to read that sentence again."

Most importantly, help make reading fun! Provide a good example for your child by letting him or her see you read, reread, and make mistakes. Talk to your child about what he or she is reading and what you have read.

Sincerely,

Getting Your Child to Love Reading

Dear Families,

It is my goal not just to teach your child to read or read better, but also to help them love reading as well. It is heartbreaking to see a child that can read choose not to read. Here are some hints for turning on a reluctant reader to the wonderful joys of reading.

1. **Read aloud, read aloud, read aloud!** It does not matter how old your child is; he or she still loves to hear stories read out loud. Seeing you get excited and emotional over a book will make him or her eager to read on his or her own. Don't be surprised if your child asks you to do this more than once a day!
2. **Let a child read what interests him or her.** This sounds simple enough, but often we read to children what we think they want to read. Go to the library or bookstore and really let them explore. Talk to your child about his or her interests, and try to find books based on that. Reading material may vary from picture books, chapter books, comics, to even cookbooks! Get that book in your child's hands, and watch him or her read!
3. **Get caught reading!** Let your child see in you what you want to see in him or her—a lifelong reader. Let your child see you reading your latest novel, the newspaper, or a favorite magazine. Children need to see what reading for enjoyment looks like. Share with them what reading is like for you.
4. **Try books on tape.** This is a great way to spend a long car ride, and you can check out many books at your local library or purchase them for a reasonable price from a book club or discount store. Individual headphones give your child the flexibility to read almost anywhere, anytime!
5. **Make reading a happy time.** Reading should be associated with pleasure, not punishment. Every book your child works through builds up their "reading miles," and makes him or her a better, more confident reader. Often, this takes time. Encouraging your child to reread familiar, safe books will give him or her the confidence needed to try new stories and text types.

Sincerely,

Questioning Your Child to Learn

Dear Families,

The kinds of questions we ask our children can help them extend and develop their learning. Here is a list to help you model questions children should ask themselves during reading. This list will also help you gain perspective on your child's understanding of the book he or she is reading.

Getting kids to ask questions before, during, and after they read will really aid them in comprehending the story. If you ask questions during the reading process, you will be modeling a necessary and essential skill for your child, a skill he or she will use in all learning situations.

Sincerely,

What

What will happen next?
What is the story about?
What did the author intend by ________?
What was the most fascinating part? Most intriguing? Most confusing?
What if ________ happened first?
What would you have written?
What would you have changed or kept the same?

Where

Where did the event happen?
Where could you find the answer?
Where would you have taken the story?
Where is the most ideal place for this story to have taken place?
Where do you see the story going? Should there be a sequel?
Where was the most interesting point for you?
Where did the author surprise you?
Where could you find more information about ________?
Where would you go next?

Why

Why did the author choose those characters and not ________?
Why do you think ________ took place first/last?
Why do you think the author included ________?
Why did the author choose the title?

How

How would you have ended this story?
How did you like the book?
How did the pictures/captions/diagrams help you?

Who

Who was most interesting to you? Why?
Who was this book intended for?
Who would you share this book with? Who would it speak to or interest most?
Who could help you find out more information about ________?
Who knows about ________?
Who is the most influential character?
Who do you most relate to in the story?
Who do you think would find the book funny? Entertaining? Confusing? Amusing?

A Book of My Own

Dear Families,

Your child is more likely to be an excited and avid reader if he or she owns books. There is a special pleasure in being able to go to your own shelf or book box and choose your favorite story. Books are wonderful but often expensive treasures, so here are a few tips for building your own home library without costing a fortune:

1. Look for the paperback version of a story. Paperback books are becoming more available. You are not sacrificing quality; you are just cutting the price in half. You can find many of your favorite titles in paperback. Be sure to ask at your bookstore if a title is available in both the hardcover and paperback. Often the display will be hardcover, but the book can be ordered in paperback.
2. There are endless finds and treasures to be found at yard sales, if you have the time. Often books are priced for less than a dollar.
3. Discount bookstores often buy, sell, and trade books of all types. You can receive up to half the selling price on many titles.
4. Most bookstore chains have a table or place in the store where they sell books at discount prices. With a little digging, you can find wonderful stories—even in hardcover versions—at a fraction of the price.
5. There is no greater gift than a cherished book given with love by a friend or family member. Each gift signifies a special memory of time together. Request that books be a part of a holiday or birthday list rather than candy or toys. Your child will welcome these special gifts.
6. Visit the library often to browse and explore all that is offered. An added bonus is that most public libraries "clean house" and discard or sell at a very reasonable price many magazines, books, novels, and overstocked inventory to make way for new merchandise.
7. There are many book clubs from which to choose, both at school and home. Many offer a variety of books at discounted prices. Make sure you read the fine print of private companies. Often they have an introductory offer and then require you to purchase a set amount of books over an extended period of time.

Sincerely,

The Kitchen Stool

Dear Families,

Your kitchen is one of the richest learning environments in your house. The next time you cook dinner, think about all of the learning opportunities there are for you and your child. Here are just a few.

1. Magnetic letters on the refrigerator can offer spelling practice.
2. Measuring cups help teach fractions.
3. Recipes offer new vocabulary and lessons in following a sequence.
4. Grocery lists show that real writers make lists to help them organize and remember things.
5. Raisins, cereal, and marshmallows can be used in estimation games.
6. Weekly coupons are great for a lesson about money.
7. Unloading and sorting the dishwasher can be an experience in counting and classification.

Try some of these, and share your ideas with me. Discover new learning in other rooms of your house as well. I am anxious to see what you come up with!

Sincerely,

Little Things Mean a Lot

Dear Families,

Remember that the little things we do for our children make a big difference. These little things cost no money and take little time, but are so necessary for your child's growth and development. Here are just a few extra ways you can help make your child feel special.

- Listen and talk to your child. Ask "What do you think?"
- Start your evening by saying "Tell me about it."
- Take a walk together.
- Make your child's favorite dinner.
- Take over one of your child's chores for the day.
- Watch your child's TV program with him or her.
- Revisit your family photo album with your child.
- Pat your child on the back for a job well done.
- Hug your child, and let him or her let go first.
- Send your child a note in his or her backpack or lunch.

You are the most important people in your child's life. Enjoy this time together!

Sincerely,

Story Staircase

Dear Families,

Telling stories can be great fun at home. Try this exciting way to build a tall, taller, and tallest tale with your child. Begin with a story starter such as one of these.

Once upon a time . . .
In a far away land . . .
Once there was a . . .
Long ago . . .
Before there was . . .
Once when there were . . .
It began when . . .

Your child adds the next line or phrase, and then you build on his or her line, and your tale will just keep growing! You may end up with something as silly as this:

Parent: *In a far away land . . .*
Child: *There lived a dragon . . .*
Parent: *Whose name was Sam . . .*
Child: *Who had a cow . . .*
Parent: *Whose name was Pam . . .*
(Just keep building, one step at a time!)

Once you have created this magnificent story, you can enjoy writing a book version with illustrations to match. What fun and laughs you will have in store—all the while, supporting your child's literacy!

Sincerely,

Homework Hints

Dear Families,

Education is important to your child's growth and development, and homework is a part of it. Here are some hints to make the "homework battle" as easy as possible.

Helping your child with this is important in setting the tone and expectation for learning. These attitudes and behaviors really make a difference at school. Thank you for your help. If you have any questions or concerns about your child's homework, please don't hesitate to call me.

Sincerely,

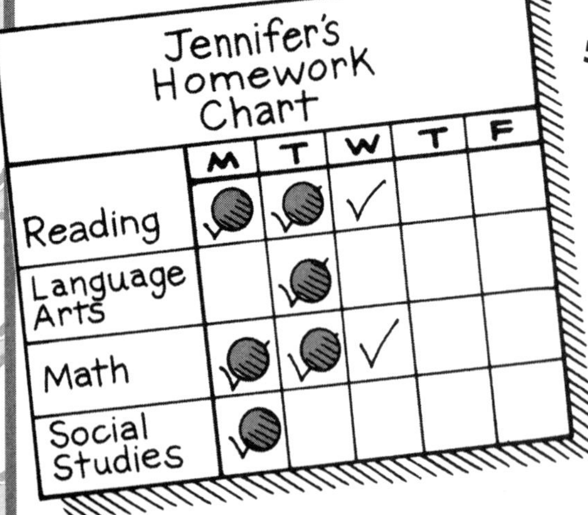

1. First, talk to your child about homework. Does your child need help? Is there adequate time to do what is required? What is going well? What can be adjusted in the schedule?

2. Have your child create a homework chart, listing all the subject areas and the days of the week. Each day after school, help your child check each box in which there is an assignment. Place a sticker or mark in a spot when the homework is complete. This is a great way for your child to take responsibility for managing and organizing his or her work.

3. Have your child make a new chart each week, or you may want to cover the original chart in sticky-backed shelf paper or laminate it for future use.

4. Set aside a consistent time each night where your child can have quiet, uninterrupted time to complete assignments.

5. Find a space at home designated for school and homework. This is where all materials, backpacks, notes, and books can be kept so that nothing will get lost or misplaced. This can be a shelf in your child's room, a bookcase, or even a box. The important thing is that all materials needed for homework to be successfully completed will be in one central area.

A Place of My Own

Dear Families,

Having personal "space" is important to us all. We all need a spot to call "A Place of My Own." You can create this area with your child using the following tips:

1. Together, find a comfortable, quiet place to study. If finding that space is not possible, you can create a "Box of My Own" so that the materials travel with your child.
2. Carpet squares, a rug, or a blanket make great ways to mark your child's space. Place a table and chair on the rug, and just put them away after use.
3. Place items in the box or space that will be used only for study and quiet time. Pencils, markers, paper, and folders make good learning utensils.
4. Have your child label or mark the spot in some way, so that it becomes something special for them.
5. Encourage your child to use the space to read books, work on homework, or practice reading and writing activities.
6. Setting up this area together sends a strong message that you care and value this quality study time. Your child will be more likely to use the space because creating it was a special event for the two of you.

Happy studying!

Sincerely,

Toys for Literacy

Dear Families,

Learning to read and write is one of the most exciting things in your child's life. Here are some toys and games that you can use at home to extend your child's learning.

1. **Magnetic Letters.** Magnetic letters can turn a simple refrigerator door into an area for spelling experimentation and sentence building. There are many styles and types available. Mix them for more visual interest.
2. **Puppets.** Handmade or from the store, puppets are great tools for the imagination. They are ideal for creating original stories and plays that you and your child can share.
3. **Tabletop Easel.** This is a wonderful tool for aspiring young artists. Many easels include a double-sided chalk or dry-erase board and come equipped with spots for paints and brushes. Most are relatively small and fold away for easy storage. With a little water and color, imaginations can bloom.
4. **ABC Puzzles.** Wooden and plastic letters introduce your child to letter-sound relationships while helping him or her learn the ABCs.

Sincerely,

On the Day You Were Born

Dear Families,

We have just finished reading the picture book, *On the Day You Were Born* by Debra Fraiser. The students loved this special story, and I would love to hear more from you about this very special day. We are creating a family display about the day the children were born. Would you take a few minutes this week to write or illustrate that memory for your child to share? We will be making a special display in our classroom to represent that special day.

You may share this day with us in any way you wish. Here are some possible ideas.

1. **Write a poem.**
2. **Draw a picture.**
3. **Share a photograph.**
4. **Write a letter to your child.**
5. **Share a funny story about the day or event.**
6. **Choose your own way!**

We are really looking forward to learning more about you and your child during the creation of this very special display!

Sincerely,

5 Conference Time

For parents and teachers alike, a parent-teacher conference can be a stressful event filled with anxiety and insecurity. Regular parent-teacher conferences for all families are an essential building block of home-school communication. Parents provide perspectives and information that can be extremely valuable to teachers. Conferences are a time for listening and mutual sharing. They reinforce the idea of working as a team.

Here are a few simple techniques to use in planning and conducting these important and necessary meetings.

1. Keep the lines of communication open and flowing.
2. Share student successes.
3. Work through concerns as a "team" with the same objective.
4. Make conferences concise and functional.
5. Keep expectations realistic and achievable. Parents won't feel as overwhelmed if they leave the conference with concrete, functional ways to help their child.
6. This is a time to talk with, not at, parents. It is understandable to want to get everything "covered"; be cautious and aware of balance.
7. Create a climate that invites collaboration with parents.
8. Establish rapport with parents and invite their unique perspectives.
9. Prioritize and set goals for continued student success.
10. Provide resources, materials, and support for families to use at home.

Getting Started

Keeping the above points in mind, use the Conference Checklist on page 71 to prepare for your parent-teacher conferences. This chapter also includes a letter to send to your parents to let them know about upcoming conference times. When you are ready to begin planning, the following "extras" will help make your conferences memorable:

1. **Student-made Invitations.** Have your students brainstorm and create special invitations as they prepare for their parents to attend. This will not only inform parents of the necessary time and date information, but it will send a message that their attendance is important for their child as well.
2. **Look Mom, I'm on TV!** Several weeks before the conference, videotape the students working in their classroom in various learning activities. Tape students over several days engaging in multiple literacy tasks. Set up a TV and VCR in the waiting area before conferences, and play the tape while parents wait for the meeting to begin. Parents love to view their child on tape, and it also lets them see what is happening

in your classroom. After conferences are completed, allow parents to check out the tape. They enjoy the opportunity to share special parts of their child's year with other family members and friends. It is a great conversation starter.

3. **Conference Take-Home Bags.** Parents are eager and anxious for specific, concrete activities that they can use with their child to help with learning at home. Choose one skill or strategy that you want parents to help reinforce at home. Create a small bag of materials and specific directions for parents and students to use the materials. At right are two samples.

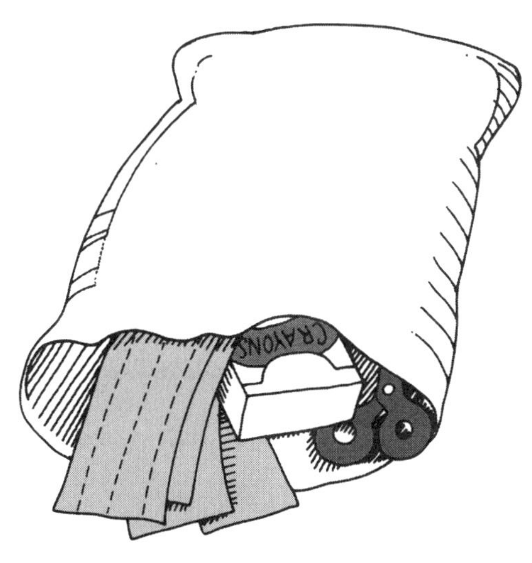

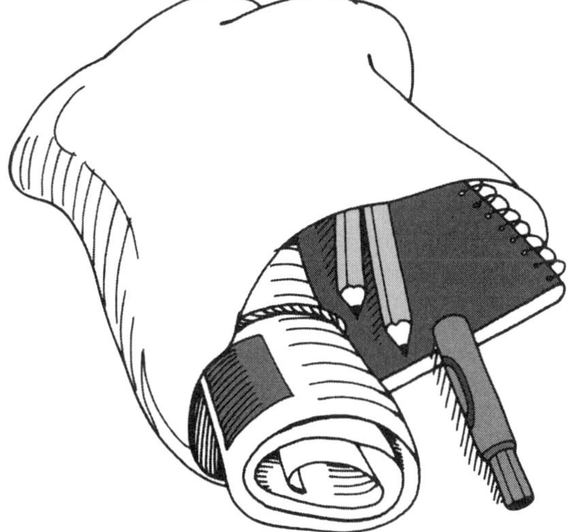

Sample Conference Bag (K, 1): **Create a Name Puzzle**

Skill Reinforced: **Name Recognition and Writing**
Bag Contents: **Sentence strips**
Small box of crayons
Scissors

Directions:

1. Print the letters of your child's name on a sentence strip.
2. Work with your child on learning the letter names and sounds that compose his or her first and last names.
3. Cut apart each of the letters, and create a puzzle for your child to practice assembling.
4. Use the extra strips to create name puzzles for other members of your family.

Sample Conference Bag (2, 3): **Words in the News**

Skill Reinforced: **Word Identification Strategies**
Bag Contents: **Newspaper or magazine**
Highlight marker
Spiral notebook
Pencils

Directions:

1. Each day choose a word or small list of words from your child's spelling list.
2. Tell your child that he or she is going to find words that he or she will need to know for reading and writing.
3. Have your child highlight the word every time he or she sees it in a newspaper or magazine.
4. Use the spiral notebook as a journal to share words that your child can recognize automatically in print.
5. You may vary this activity in several ways: try looking for compound words, plurals, adjectives, adverbs, etc.

When Conflicts Arise

Your goal will always be to be proactive, but there may come a time when the lines of communication break down and a conflict arises. It is important to remember the following tips when dealing with a defensive or angry parent.

1. Parents and teachers have a limited number of contacts during the year. This places a lot of pressure on both when they do take place. Each has their own agenda, beliefs, and feelings.
2. Many parents have negative or uncomfortable associations about schools because of their own experiences or prior contacts.
3. Roles are changing. There is a question of who is responsible for what aspects of the child's life. Lines are often blurred. A child often acts differently with the teacher than at home with the parents. Both perspectives are necessary and needed when working out a common understanding.

Keep "cool under pressure"

- Stay calm and collected.
- Don't assume anything.
- Put yourself in the parent's place.
- Be prepared and have documentation.
- Understand parent expectations and be sure they understand yours.
- Don't make promises you are unable to keep.
- Know your limits–the child is ultimately the parent's responsibility.
- Call for assistance, if necessary.
- Listen, listen, listen. Often parents just need a few moments to vent. Once this is done, then they are more willing to talk things out.

Remember: You may not always see eye to eye, but you can try to reach parents heart to heart. Keep in mind that you both have the child's best interest at heart.

Conference Planning Checklist

Planning ahead to ensure a successful conference is crucial. This before-conference preparation will set the tone for the meeting and, often, for future contacts. The following checklist will help you organize and prepare for the day.

Before the Conference

- ☐ Send home pre-conference note (see sample on page 72). You may want to include a reminder of the time and date for the scheduled conference at this time. You may also wish to send home the "10 Steps to a Successful Conference" checklist (page 72) with the pre-conference note.
- ☐ Display parent sign-up sheet for times.
- ☐ Display the time and date and other notes on the bulletin board.
- ☐ Send home the input sheet with information you want parents to bring to the conference.
- ☐ Create an agenda of what is to be discussed.
- ☐ Develop a flexible schedule that provides multiple options for attendance.
- ☐ Contact parents in advance to confirm and remind them of the conference date.
- ☐ Check that student work is displayed.
- ☐ Inspect the classroom; is it organized and clean?
- ☐ Make available adult-sized chairs and tables; be sure that no desk separates you from the parents.
- ☐ Prepare the waiting area with student books, photos, magazines, etc.
- ☐ Welcome the parents who arrive early.

During the Conference

- ☐ Set and share agenda.
- ☐ Begin with the parent sharing information on the input sheet.
- ☐ Start with the families' questions that can be answered throughout the conference. (If answering the questions a parent raises extends the conference past the allotted time, invite that parent to discuss the issues at a separate date and time.)
- ☐ Share concrete examples of student work and assessments. (A nice range of early, middle, and current work is very effective in showing student growth.)
- ☐ Discuss report card/grading system.
- ☐ Discuss goals for the student at home and school. (You can set student goals together.)
- ☐ Discuss final thoughts and questions.

After the Conference

- ☐ Keep notes about the conference; follow through and remember parents' concerns.
- ☐ Keep parents informed of any steps or actions taken as a result of the conference.
- ☐ If necessary, contact other school staff when issues arise that concern them.

Above all, *start and end on a positive note!*

Conference Time

Dear Families,

Conference time is just around the corner. I am looking forward to sharing your child's progress and successes with you. I want this to be a time for you to ask questions and share your insights. Below is a brief chart, "10 Steps to a Successful Conference." I hope it helps spark ideas and thoughts for you to share. I am looking forward to seeing you all.

Sincerely,

10 Steps to a Successful Conference

1. Get to know the teacher early in the school year. The earlier the contact, the better the chance of setting up a good communication channel.
2. Plan ahead. Talk to your child and jot down any questions you have. Review your child's books and recent homework assignments.
3. If both parents or caregivers are available, attend the conference either together or schedule separately. The greater the number of significant adults sharing information and supporting the student, the more success the student can attain.
4. Feel free to ask questions. Your questions will be important in helping the lines of communication stay open and flowing.
5. Share any information that may help the teacher develop a better understanding of your child.
6. Talk with your child before and after the conference to share with him or her what was discussed and shared.
7. Decide together what, if anything, needs to be done to support your child further. Agree on a plan and on any special assistance your child may need before you leave.
8. Follow up. Implement the suggested support from home, and keep in touch with the school on how things are progressing. If the agreed-upon plan is not working, or if new or different problems develop, feel free to call and ask for another meeting.
9. Ask for additional help if you feel that you need it. The teacher is there to support any and all that you are doing at home. If I can be of further help, please let me know.
10. If problems do arise, please contact the teacher as soon as possible. You do not need a formally scheduled conference to work out a question or problem. Communication is what will make this partnership successful.

6 Literacy on the Go

A Collection of Learning Games

Understanding that there are many kinds of literacy is key to developing programs with families. The use of reading and writing within family contexts does not necessarily reflect the teaching of reading and writing in the classroom or school (Taylor, 1999). There is no single way to become literate. Each family literacy experience is different and can be encouraged and validated. There is a tendency for many parent involvement programs to focus on storybook reading alone. The games in this chapter can help children and parents become involved in multiple literacy events throughout the day. These practical literacy games help parents capitalize on the opportunity to build, discover, and explore literacy and the language all around them. We must understand that time is a precious commodity for families. Parents can use these games literally anytime. They can provide parents with tools for literacy conversation while doing everyday tasks, such as going to the grocery store or riding in the car to and from school.

The following literacy games give parents practical ideas to support their child's literacy development at home. Stress to parents that there is no one way to play them. Encourage families to make adaptations and changes that suit their child's needs. You can copy the games onto cardstock, punch a hold in them, and bind them together with a metal ring so that they are easily accessible to busy families. They are designed to fit in a bag, purse, glove box, or in a small space at home for quick reference. Here are some suggestions for sharing the games with families in your classroom.

Suggestions for sharing the games:

1. Reproduce the games as shown and share them with families at a conference or open house or a similar parent event.

2. Create a parent workshop using the literacy game format. Invite the parents to school and discuss how they use reading and writing in their everyday lives. Play some of the games and discuss the value of these everyday literacy opportunities. Then have parents form an assembly line and create the booklets for their home use.

3. You may want to share these functional games with just one or two families who are struggling to find time to read to their child each night. You can explain that talking with your children about literacy in an everyday context is a wonderful and powerful way to support literacy development.

4. Share these functional literacy games at your school, and brainstorm, with your colleagues or teachers at your grade level, other games to add.

5. After sharing the games with parents, send a follow-up letter home asking for their feedback and other ways they are engaging in literacy conversation with their child. Share feedback with all the families, and add to the collection. It will validate what parents are doing at home and can become a bridge between home and school literacy.

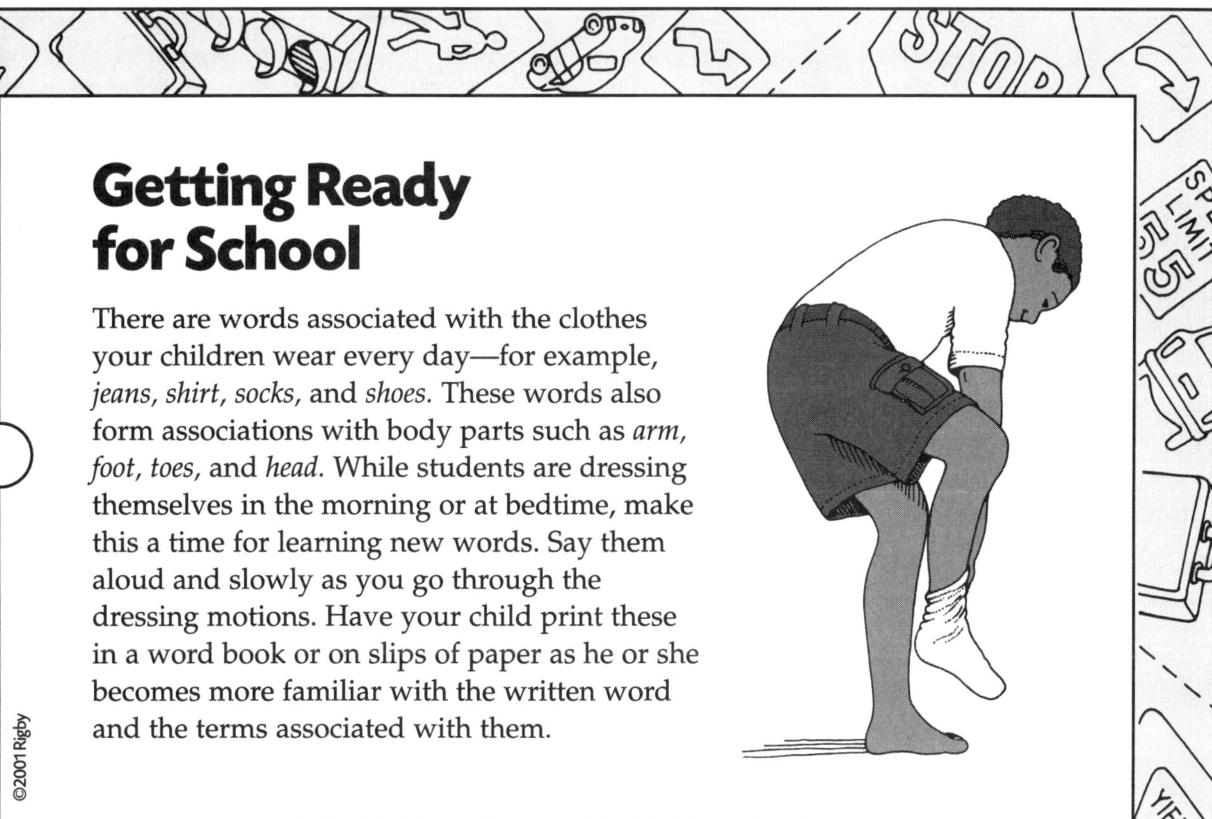

Getting Ready for School

There are words associated with the clothes your children wear every day—for example, *jeans, shirt, socks,* and *shoes.* These words also form associations with body parts such as *arm, foot, toes,* and *head.* While students are dressing themselves in the morning or at bedtime, make this a time for learning new words. Say them aloud and slowly as you go through the dressing motions. Have your child print these in a word book or on slips of paper as he or she becomes more familiar with the written word and the terms associated with them.

Rhymes All Around!

Everywhere we go, rhymes are all around. Take a trip in the car, to the grocery store, or around your house and say rhyming words with your child.

For example

Car: *tire/fire, door/floor, mat/fat, key/see*

Grocery Store: *bag/sag, eat/feet, aisle/file, cart/smart, shop/hop*

Bedroom: *bed/head, light/night, sock/clock*

Kitchen: *spoon/moon, plate/gate, glass/bass*

You can play this rhyming game anywhere. If your child would like to record these newfound rhymes, have a blank spiral notebook available to write the rhyming words for each room or place discussed.

Word Hunt

Words and language surround us. Go on a "Word Hunt" in your house. Look for words that are represented in each room of your house. Get a large piece of posterboard and draw an outline of your home or apartment, labeling the areas for kitchen, garage, bedroom, bathroom, etc. The "Word Hunt" is ready to begin! Each night pick a separate room to explore, and have your child write down all of the words that he or she finds in that room. See the box at right for examples.

Kitchen:
refrigerator, stove, butter, cookbook, ketchup

Bathroom:
toilet paper, bubbles, deodorant, hairspray

Making Labels

In many elementary classrooms, labeling classroom objects is a wonderful literacy learning tool. You can extend this learning to your home. At school children label desks and tables; at home a child can label his or her bed, rooms of the house, toys, and materials. Masking tape or sticky notes work well and leave no damaging marks on the furniture and are easily removed.

I Spy at the Grocery Store

Playing "I Spy" has never been so fun with all the items available at the local grocery. Begin with simple clues, and get increasingly difficult as your child becomes familiar with the pattern. Bring in concepts of color, shape, letter and sound knowledge, comparison, and predictions. These are great skills to reinforce all the while you are shopping for items on your grocery list.

I spy something that is oval and starts with *e*–**eggs!**

I spy something that is green and crunchy and starts the same as licorice–**lettuce.**

I spy something that is liquid and ends with a *k* sound–**milk**

I spy something that rhymes with *red* and starts like brick–**bread.**

Tell Me a Story

Reading is so important that we must make time every day. If there is no time to sit down with a storybook, telling a story is a powerful way to share literacy with your child. Here are a few simple story starters to get you thinking:

When I was six . . .

The day I was sad . . .

I remember . . .

My favorite place in the world is . . .

On the day you were born . . .

I am feeling happy . . .

I am the greatest . . .

One time I got in trouble for doing . . .

Storytelling Twisters

Anytime can be story time: on your way to school, waiting for an appointment, riding in the car, or right before going to bed. Try creating a new version of one of your favorite tales and stories. Have your child make up a new ending to a familiar story. The following are good starts. Within each story a problem arises, and this makes for interesting conversation as you question aloud how the problem might be solved differently.

- Goldilocks and the Three Bears
- Cinderella
- Jack and the Beanstalk
- Snow White

Follow-up Suggestions: New endings will give many of these tales and stories a twist. These new stories would make fun read-alouds to share and compare with your child.

Signs and Sounds

As you are riding with your child in the car, take time to point out the signs you encounter. Bring to your child's attention the letter and sound that each sign represents.

For example

S for stop sign
B for bank, barber
F for fire station

When children develop an association with these very familiar objects in their everyday environment, learning the letter names and sounds will become an easier task.

Message Maker

You are your child's first and most important model for reading and writing. Start a tradition of showing him or her writing as a communication tool by exchanging notes with one another. Make a point one or two times a week to leave a note on a sticky tag in a very special place (the lunchbox, on a pillow, the bathroom mirror). Write the message so that your child can read it. Give your child a pad of stickytags, and encourage him or her to surprise you with a return message.

I'm always thinking of you! Love, Mom

Little ______ Muffet

Nursery Rhymes are a wonderful way to increase your child's vocabulary and to help them see the rhyme and rhythm of language. This is a fun on-the-go activity to do with your child anytime, anywhere. Begin to share an entire nursery rhyme with your child. After you have read, sung, or said the nursery rhyme once, go through the rhyme again, intentionally leaving out words and, eventually, phrases. Have your child "fill in the blanks" to complete the rhyme.

Parent: Little Miss Muffet sat on a

tuffet eating her curds and *(whey)* CHILD

along came a *(spider)* CHILD

who sat down *(beside)* CHILD her

and *(frightened Miss Muffet away!)* CHILD

Rhyme Refresher

Here is a quick review of some old favorites.

Mary Had a Little Lamb
Mary had a little lamb,
Little lamb, little lamb.
Mary had a little lamb
Whose fleece was white as snow.

Humpty Dumpty
Humpty Dumpty sat on a wall.
Humpty Dumpty had a great fall.
All the king's horses and all the king's men,
Couldn't put Humpty together again.

Jack and Jill
Jack and Jill went up the hill
to fetch a pail of water.
Jack fell down and broke his crown.
And Jill came tumbling after.

Old King Cole
Old King Cole was merry old soul,
And a merry old soul was he.
He called for his pipe and he called for his bowl,
And he called for his fiddlers three.

Reading the Paper

As you browse through the newspaper, have your child sit alongside you. You are giving him or her an excellent model of reading. As you finish each section, have your child join in with some of these simple and fun activities.

1. Highlight words he or she will see over and over in his or her own reading and writing. These are words such as *the, and, is, can, are,* and *on.* When your child can recognize this core of words automatically, he or she will be able to read more difficult material at a more successful rate. It may help to highlight just one or two words a day. For example, have your child mark all the times that he or she sees *the* in the sports section. Tomorrow try the word *and* in the comics, and so on.
2. You can also have your child find specific letters. It works well to start with the letters in his or her name because those will be most familiar.
3. Practice reading parts of the paper. Discuss captions, headlines, comics, editorials, etc.

Emergency Literacy Kit

Just as you may have an emergency kit in your car with items you would need if you ran into trouble on the road, you can create an "Emergency Literacy Kit" to keep in the car or to carry on the train or bus. The items you choose should reflect your child's interests and needs. A small backpack or bag with a zipper works well. If you set the kit down or tip it over during a ride, you don't need to worry about spills and messes. Here are some ideas on how to stock the kit.

Sample Kit Materials

A favorite reading or bedtime book	Colored pencils	Travel games
Spiral notebook or journal	Crayons	Sticky notes
Pencils	Markers	Glue stick
	Stickers	Scissors (plastic-edged for safety)
	Headphones with books on tape	

The kit can change over time, and you can add new things as your child's literacy needs change. Making the kit together can be a special time to show your child how you value literacy.

Silverware Sort

Make your everyday household tasks a learning event. Unloading the dishwasher has never been this fun. Have your child write the contents of the dishwasher on 3-inch-x-5-inch index cards (plates, forks, knives, cups, bowls). Don't worry about spelling; let your child create the labels that make sense to him or her. After the labels are done, let the sorting begin! As you unload, have you child match and stack up the appropriate dishes and utensils in the correct spot. This is not just a great reading and writing activity, but it also helps with sorting and classification. The added bonus is that the dishes are done! You can also play this game with laundry and label socks, pants, shirts, and so on.

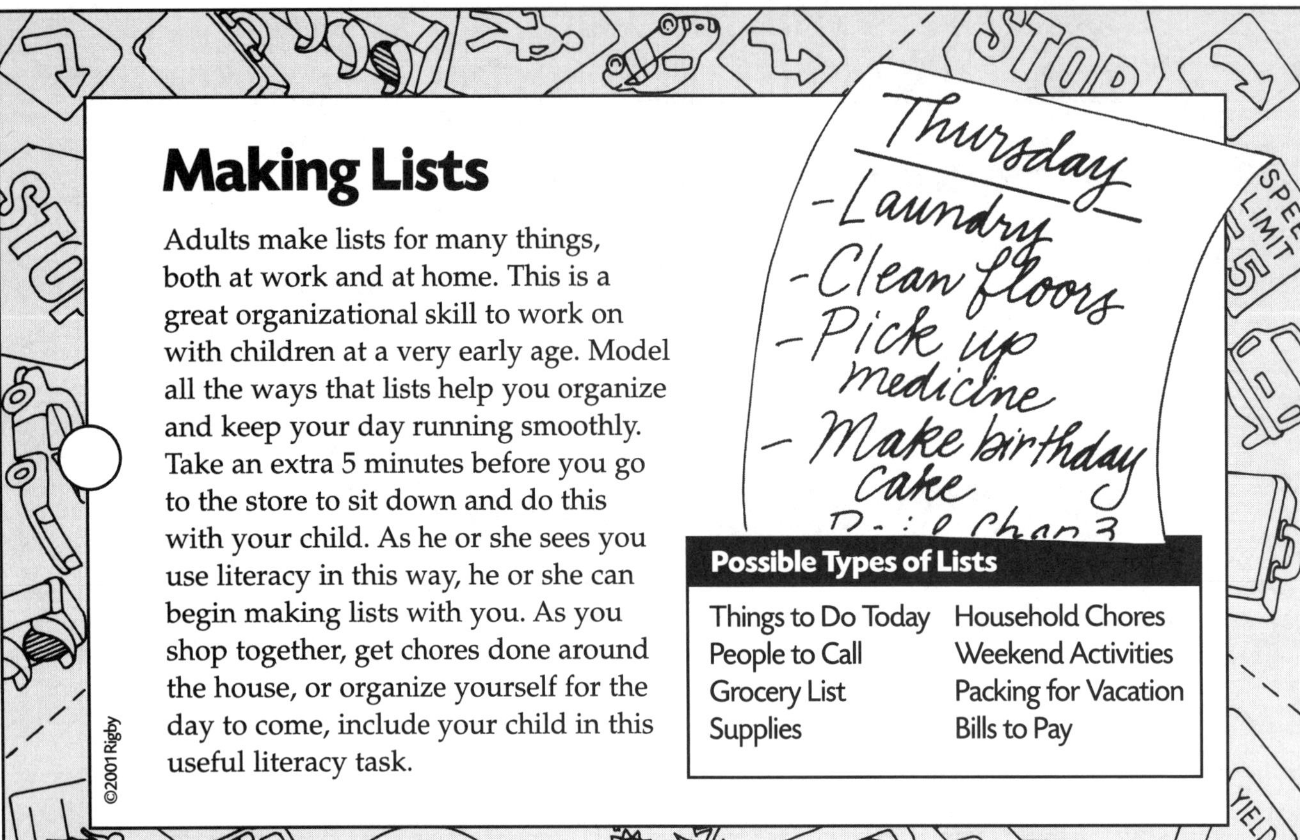

Making Lists

Adults make lists for many things, both at work and at home. This is a great organizational skill to work on with children at a very early age. Model all the ways that lists help you organize and keep your day running smoothly. Take an extra 5 minutes before you go to the store to sit down and do this with your child. As he or she sees you use literacy in this way, he or she can begin making lists with you. As you shop together, get chores done around the house, or organize yourself for the day to come, include your child in this useful literacy task.

Possible Types of Lists

Things to Do Today	Household Chores
People to Call	Weekend Activities
Grocery List	Packing for Vacation
Supplies	Bills to Pay

Environmental Print Walk

Some of the first words your child learns to read are names of fast-food restaurants and popular stores or soft drinks. This "environmental print" surrounds us. Take a walk in your neighborhood and bring along a journal. Record all of the signs, buildings, and restaurants that are around you daily. Help your child make connections to these familiar words to build on when they are learning new words. For example, if you and your child were reading the sentence, "I can make a rainbow," and your child got stuck on the word *make,* you could remind him or her that the word starts with the same sound as the name of his or her favorite fast-food restaurant.

Dear Diary

Begin to keep a family diary to record special events in your lives (events of your day, parties, birthdays, or vacations). Have your child help you make the record, sharing stories and memories along the way. Your child may be so excited about the process that he or she may want to begin a diary.

Hidden Letters

All around the kitchen, from the cupboard to the stove, there are letters. There are *b*s and *c*s and *f*s and *g*s. They are located on cereal boxes, food bags, and cans. Make a game finding these letters. Tell your child to find 6 *A*s or 14 *B*s. Have him or her look for combinations of the letters. Your child can write down all the letters he or she has discovered, and you will have been able to cook dinner in peace!

Give Me an *A*

While you are out walking, driving, or sitting in the yard playing, try this game. Ask your child to observe as many things that begin with the letter you call out. You will be surprised at how challenging this may be. Your child will really enjoy this upbeat way of observing and describing the world around him or her. For example, if you are outside playing "Give Me a *B*," your child might say: ball, bumblebee, bicycle, brick, ball, bird, brown shirt, or berries on a tree.

The Learning Toolbox

Children are naturally curious. It is important to foster that interest to keep learning alive for your child. The learning toolbox is a special box in which to keep interesting items for your child to experiment with. Materials can be changed often and can be added at the request of your child based on his or her learning needs.

Here are some ideas to get you started.

Box Ideas

Ribbons	Clay
Cotton swabs	Glitter
Sandpaper	Writing materials: pencils, crayons, markers
Chalk	Sticky notes
Pipe cleaners	
Metal fasteners	

1. Get a box with an attached lid.
2. Decorate the box with your child, and label it the "Learning Toolbox."
3. Fill the box with five or six items that are ready for experimentation. There is no right or wrong thing to place in the box—the more unique something is, the better.

©2001 Rigby

License to Read

We all remember playing the license-plate game. What a wonderful learning opportunity it can be, as children identify states by colors, letters, and numbers. Have your child try the following activities.

1. Tally all of the plates from the different states. Keep a record and compare the numbers.
2. Find the letters in your name or your family names.
3. After you are home, design your own new state plate. What would be a good representation of the state in which you live? What color? What shape? What pictures would you include?
4. Keep a record of the most unique personalized plates. Which were funny? Silly? Confusing?

Roadside ABCs "Plus"

Here are some additions to the great roadside alphabet game. This is one of the best ways to reinforce letter-sound relationships and is guaranteed to make the ride to grandmother's house go smoothly and quickly! Try it the traditional way: Have your child keep a record of all he or she sees that starts with the letters of the alphabet. For example: *A* apple tree, *B* branch, *C* cow, or *D* driveway. Do this mentally or keep a tally on a notepad. If more than one child is playing, it is fun to have a contest and see who can complete the task first.

Following are a few variations of this game:

- Try the same game, but start with *Z* and work your way backward through the alphabet.
- Do the vowels first, and then move on to the consonants.
- You find the even letters, and have your child find the odd ones. For example: You do *A*, *C*, *E*, *G*, *I*, and your child looks for *B*, *D*, *F*, and *H*.
- Find objects that start with the letters in your child's name. Then move to his or her middle name, last name, family members' names, etc. You will not only be working on alphabet knowledge but spelling as well!

Creating a Pizza Portfolio

Here is a great way to store all of the many treasures that a child brings home to share. Ask your local pizza merchant for several extra pizza boxes. They are really willing to share and cost little or nothing.

Have families decorate the outside of the box with sticky-backed shelf paper or construction paper. Label the box with your child's name, the school year, and the grade level your child is in. Each month, have each child select special pieces or projects that will be kept.

The boxes stack well and can be easily stored. Use packaging tape to reinforce the ends so they will stand the test of time. Parents will enjoy wonderful conversations with their children as they select their treasures.

Helping Your Child with Patterns

The ability to create a pattern is an early math skill that you can encourage in your child. Patterns occur throughout mathematics. Using objects rather than numbers is your first step in helping your child discover that patterns are truly everywhere. Many objects at home can be used to create a pattern. Here are just a few.

1. **Fruit Cereal Rings:** red, yellow, red, yellow
2. **Silverware:** fork, spoon, fork, spoon
3. **Laundry:** shirt, socks, pants, shirt, socks, pants
4. **Writing Tools:** pencil, pen, marker, crayon, pencil, pen, marker, crayon

Your child should begin by finishing a pattern you have started. As he or she masters the "two-object" pattern (known as AB patterning), add a third (ABC, ABC, ABC), and a fourth (ABCD, ABCD, ABCD).

7 Let's Cook!

Have you have ever cooked with the children in your classroom? If so, you know what an exciting learning event this can be. Children love to mix, stir, and create masterful treats. Cooking is not only fun for students, but the time spent during the cooking process is full of wonderful learning opportunities. Students are learning the math skills of measurement, fractions, sequencing, and division. They are engaged in meaningful, real-life reading and writing as you work through the recipes together.

Cooking is also a wonderful way to bridge the learning between school and home. Families must eat every day. We can share with them all the learning opportunities available to them as they cook with their children at home. Not only can this be a time for us to share helpful ideas with parents, but we can invite their expertise in as well.

Here are some ways families can be involved in cooking projects both at home or at school.

1. Plan a special day in your classroom to cook up a treat with students. This could be in response to a book read aloud, a special celebration, or just for fun. Invite parents to assist with the process. You can get them involved by having each family bring in one item to complete the cooking project. Model for them all of the learning skills involved in this exciting activity.
2. You can send the letters and recipes home to parents who might like to cook with their child. Each family can prepare its special treat, and students can tell all about the experience at school.
3. Cooking is a great way for families to share their culture and tradition. Invite parents in to make a special family recipe with the class. This will provide learning opportunities about the skills involved in preparing the recipe, but also about various histories of the families in your classroom.

The letters in this chapter include an introduction for parents, as well as a list of cooking terms and a poster with safety tips. The recipes in this chapter are designed to be used in multiple ways with students at all levels. Families will love to be involved in this learning process. The following recipes have been designed to send home to parents in several formats.

1. You may want to consider inviting parents into your classroom for a demonstration workshop on using the recipes. It is not only the cooking that provides a learning opportunity, but also the conversation that surrounds the event. You want to model reading the recipe, measuring, following the correct sequence, and all the reading and writing skills involved in a cooking session.

2. If you choose to have parents cook in your classroom, have them sign up and bring in the needed supplies for the recipe. This will allow them to be a part of the workshop from the beginning. Or have each parent and child create the recipe separately. The recipes are designed with the child in mind, so the child should be doing the majority of the cooking, with some assistance from adults when necessary.

3. The recipes can also be sent in the provided format. You could also include a comment page and a blank recipe form (p. 118) so that parents can write their own versions of the recipes and reflect upon the home cooking experience.

4. You may pull the recipes from this book and three-hole punch the pages for parents' ease of use.

Cooking Your Way Through the Alphabet

- **A** Amazing Apple Salad
- **B** Banana Supreme
- **C** Creative Cookie Creations
- **D** Deliciously "Dirty" Desert
- **E** "Egg-cellent" Egg Supreme
- **F** Fancy Fruit Pizza
- **G** Great Green Treat
- **H** Happy Holiday Tree
- **I** Ice Cream Cookie Surprise
- **J** Jelly Surprise
- **K** Krazy Kabobs
- **L** Luscious Lemony Drink
- **M** Muffin Magic
- **N** Nutty Banana Pop
- **O** O. J. Plus
- **P** Pudding Parfait
- **Q** Quick-to-Fix Mix
- **R** Rocky Road Sundae
- **S** Sassy Salsa
- **T** Terrific Tacos
- **U** The "Uncola®" Float
- **V** Vanishing Veggie Treat
- **W** Wacky Wagon Wheels
- **X** "X" Marks the Spot Biscuits
- **Y** Yum Yum Desert
- **Z** Zesty Zucchini Pie

Cooking Your Way Through the Alphabet

Dear Families,

Each week I will be sending you a new recipe to cook with your child. These recipes are especially designed for each person to have his or her own portion. Learning comes from your child doing the cutting, mixing, pouring, stirring, and creating. Wonderful conversation can arise when you have both "followed the recipe," but the product turns out much different.

There is one recipe designated for each letter of the alphabet. Cooking is also a great way to reinforce both reading and writing skills.

Remember to have great fun when trying out these new dishes. The recipes require little preparation and few supplies and can be done in a short amount of time. The original recipes are prepunched and can be placed in a three ring binder or folder. You can add your family favorites to your new cookbook as well. I have also included additional pages for you and your child to create and write your own recipes! Have fun, and happy cooking!

Sincerely,

Cooking Words to Know

Dear Families,

Cooking is an amazing learning experience to share with your child. It is also a wonderful opportunity to build and develop his or her vocabulary. As you try out these recipes, please share with them the terms that go along with this process.

Beat:	To stir hard
Blend:	To mix thoroughly
Boiling:	To heat water until bubbles are popping in it
Chill:	To put in the refrigerator to cool
Chop:	To cut into small pieces
Crumble:	To break into crumbs
Crush:	To break into very small bits using a tool, such as a rolling pin
Dissolve:	To stir boiling water until crystals disappear
Stir:	To mix together with a large spoon or rubber scraper
Thaw:	To become unfrozen and soft
Wedge:	To shape like a triangle

Sincerely,

Rules of the Kitchen

1. Wash your hands with soap and water before you begin any cooking project.
2. Read the whole recipe carefully before starting.
3. Collect all of the ingredients and equipment you need for the recipe before you start to cook.
4. Do one step of the recipe at a time. Do not skip steps.
5. Measure carefully using the correct equipment.
6. Never let children use the stove, oven, or garbage disposal alone.
7. Create a "Safety Zone." Mark off a space around the stove or oven with masking tape, so your child knows how close they can be.
8. Turn pot handles toward the center of the stove or oven so that children cannot grab them and tip over the hot contents.
9. Be sure to cover electrical sockets when they are not in use.
10. Use safety guards on drawers and doors.
11. Adult supervision is recommended with even plastic knives. Children should remain sitting while doing any cutting and chopping.
12. Clean up when you are finished!
13. Share your wonderful creations with family and friends.

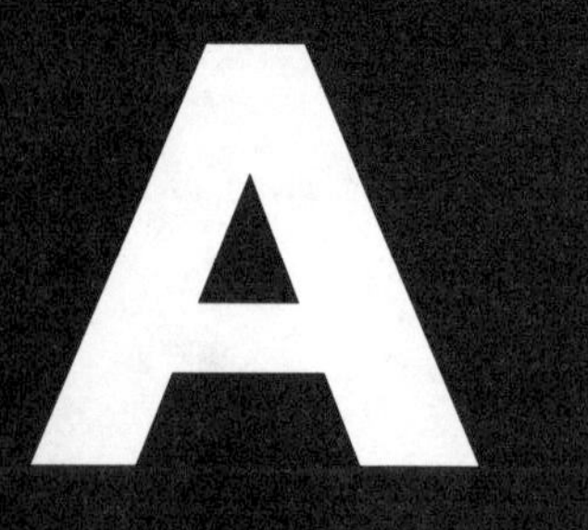

Amazing Apple Salad

Ingredients

1 medium apple (cored)
1 Tbsp. mayonnaise
1 Tbsp. marshmallows
$\frac{1}{2}$ stalk of celery
10 raisins

Supplies

Paper cups
Measuring spoons
Plastic knife and spoon

Recipe Directions

1. Cut your apple into 4 pieces.
2. Cut the apple pieces into small cubed squares.
3. Cut the celery stalk in pieces.
4. Place the apple pieces, raisins, nuts, celery, and marshmallows in your cup.
5. Add the dressing and stir.
6. You may chill your salad for 1 hour or dig in!

Banana Supreme

Ingredients

$\frac{1}{2}$ cup vanilla pudding mix
2 cups milk for pudding mix
$\frac{1}{2}$ banana sliced
2 Tbsp. crushed vanilla wafers
2 Tbsp. whipped cream topping

Supplies

Plastic spoons and cups
Measuring spoons
Measuring cups

Recipe Directions

1. Mix the pudding (use instructions on the box).
2. Pour the pudding in the plastic cup.
3. Mix the pudding and the whipped cream.
4. Mix the sliced banana with the pudding mixture.
5. Top with crushed wafer cookies.
6. Eat and enjoy!

Creative Cookie Creations

Ingredients

2 vanilla wafer cookies
1 tsp. peanut butter
1 square of vanilla almond candy coating

Supplies

1 craft stick
Wax paper
Plastic knife and spoon
Large bowl
Measuring spoons

Recipe Directions

1. Spread the peanut butter on the two wafer cookies.
2. Place the stick between the two cookies and press together.
3. Heat the candy coating until melted, stirring constantly.
4. Dip half of the cookie pop in the melted coating.
5. Place the cookie on the wax paper to cool for 5 minutes.
6. Eat and enjoy!

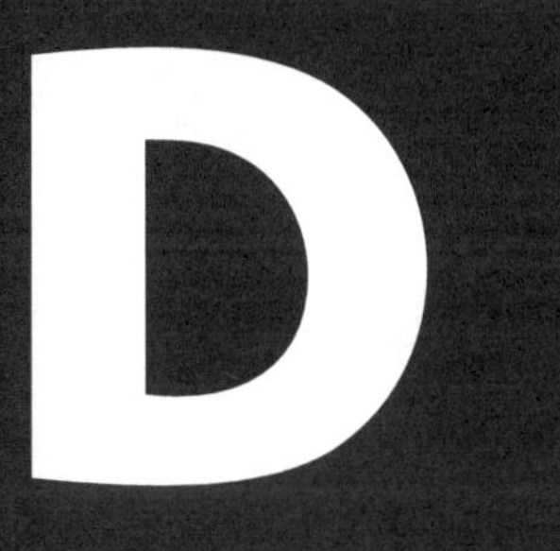

Deliciously "Dirty" Dessert

Ingredients

$\frac{1}{2}$ cup chocolate pudding mix
2 cups cold milk for the pudding mix
2 Tbsp. crushed chocolate sandwich cookies
2 Tbsp. whipped cream topping
Gummy worms (optional)

Supplies

Plastic cup and spoon
Measuring spoons
Large bowl for the pudding

Recipe Directions

1. Make the chocolate-flavored pudding with milk, as directed on the box.
2. Place $\frac{1}{2}$ cup of pudding in the plastic cup.
3. Stir in 1 tablespoon of the crushed cookies and whipped topping.
4. Top each cup of pudding mixture with the remaining crushed cookies.
5. For a more authentic "dirt" look, place the gummy worms in the pudding mixture.

E

"Egg-cellent" Egg Supreme

Ingredients

1 egg
1 Tbsp. milk
1 Tbsp. grated cheese
1 oz. cubed ham
$\frac{1}{8}$ tsp. salt
$\frac{1}{2}$ tsp. onion flakes
Cooking spray for the skillet or pan

Supplies

Plastic cup
Measuring spoons
Electric skillet

Recipe Directions

1. Spray the electric skillet with nonstick cooking spray.
2. In a plastic cup, break the egg.
3. Beat in cheese, ham, salt, and onion flakes.
4. Cook thoroughly in the skillet.
5. Serve with toast and juice. Enjoy!

Fancy Fruit Pizza

Ingredients

2 Tbsp. whipped topping
1 tube of pre-made sugar-cookie dough
4 grapes
1 strawberry
4 kiwi fruit slices
8 fresh blueberries
(Any combination of fruit may be substituted)
Nonstick cooking spray

Supplies

Plastic knife and fork
Paper plate
Measuring spoons

Recipe Directions

1. Unwrap the tube of cookie dough.
2. Cut two serving sizes and roll into a ball.
3. Pat out the dough to form a circular pizza shape.
4. Place the dough on a greased cookie sheet and bake according to package directions.
5. Let the cookie pizza base cool.
6. Frost with the whipped dairy topping and place the fruit on top.
7. Chill for one hour, and enjoy this decorative treat!

Great Green Treat

Ingredients

3 chocolate sandwich creme cookies
$\frac{1}{2}$ cup mint chocolate chip ice cream
1 Tbsp. hot fudge sauce
2 Tbsp. whipped dairy topping

Supplies

Plastic bowl and spoon
Measuring spoons and cup
Locking sandwich bag

Recipe Directions

1. Place the sandwich cookies in the plastic bag and crush into crumbs.
2. Line the bottom of the plastic bowl with cookie crumbs to form a cookie crust (reserve some for later).
3. Fill the bowl with the ice cream and press down firmly. Freeze to harden.
4. Spread hot fudge topping on the mixture.
5. Top with whipped topping and the remainder of the cookie crumbs. Serve frozen.

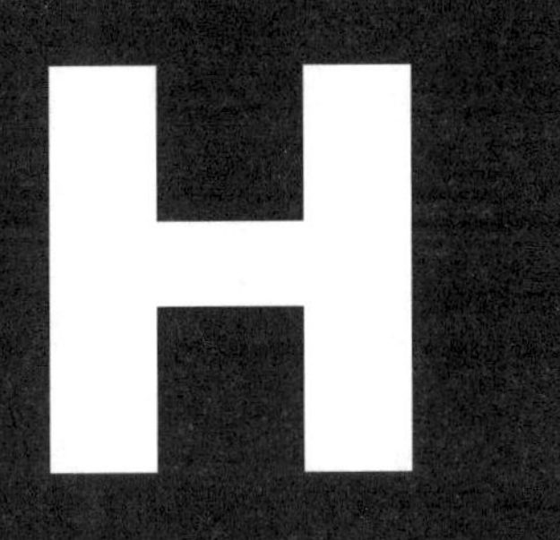

Happy Holiday Tree

Ingredients

One sugar ice cream cone
2 Tbsp. of vanilla frosting
1 graham cracker
1 Tbsp. coconut flakes
1 Tbsp. red hot candies
1 Tbsp. candy sprinkles
Green food coloring

Supplies

Plastic knife and fork
Paper plates and cups
Measuring spoons

Recipe Directions

1. Mix one drop of food coloring with the frosting in the paper cup.
2. Frost the graham cracker square with the frosting mixture and place the cone upside-down onto the cracker.
3. Spread coconut flakes on the cracker square to represent fallen snow.
4. Frost the tree with the remainder of green frosting mixture. Decorate with red hots and candies.
5. This holiday tree can be used as a decoration or you can enjoy nibbling the tasty pieces.

I

Ice Cream Cookie Surprise

Ingredients

Chocolate chip cookies (packaged will work)
$\frac{1}{2}$ cup vanilla ice cream
1 Tbsp. mini chocolate chips
1 Tbsp. hot fudge topping
1 tsp. chopped nuts

Supplies

Wax paper
Measuring spoons
Plastic knife and spoon

Recipe Directions

1. Place the $\frac{1}{2}$ cup of ice cream on the inside of one cookie.
2. Top this with the hot fudge and chopped nuts.
3. Place the second cookie on top of the mixture to form a cookie sandwich.
4. Place the chocolate chips on waxed paper.
5. Roll the cookie combination along the wax paper to cover the ice cream sides.
6. Freeze the cookie sandwich for 4 hours.
7. Thaw for 10 minutes before eating.

J

Jelly Surprise

Ingredients

2 Tbsp. jelly or jam (your favorite flavor)
2 Tbsp. peanut butter
1 Tbsp. margarine
2 slices of bread
1 marshmallow or 1 slice of banana

Supplies

Measuring spoons
Mixing bowl
Plastic knife and spoon

Recipe Directions

1. Measure and mix together all the ingredients except the bread.
2. Beat until smooth and creamy.
3. Spread on one bread slice.
4. Place marshmallow or banana slice in the middle of the spread.
5. Top your special jelly treat with the second bread slice.
6. Enjoy!

Krazy Kabobs

Ingredients

- $\frac{1}{4}$ medium apple
- 4 pineapple chunks
- 4 grapes
- 4 mini marshmallows
- $\frac{1}{4}$ banana
- 4 raisins

Supplies

- Grilling skewers or long toothpicks
- Plastic knife
- Plastic bowls

Recipe Directions

1. Cut the apple and banana into small chunks.
2. Place all of the fruits and treats in plastic bowls.
3. Assemble the ingredients onto the skewers, alternating the food (for example: apple, raisin, banana, and marshmallow).
4. Add other fruit combinations to the kabob if you wish. Veggies work great, too!

L

Luscious Lemony Drink

Ingredients

$\frac{1}{2}$ lemon
$\frac{1}{4}$ tsp. lemon juice
1 Tbsp. honey or sugar for sweetening
$\frac{1}{2}$ cup cold water
Ice cubes

Supplies

Plastic knife
Plastic cup
Straw (optional)

Recipe Directions

1. Pour the cold water into a cup.
2. Squeeze the fresh lemon into the water.
3. Add the lemon juice and sweetener to the lemon water.
4. Pour over the ice cubes and add a straw for sipping this cool, refreshing lemon drink!

Muffin Magic

Ingredients

$\frac{1}{2}$ English muffin
1 Tbsp. spaghetti sauce
2 Tbsp. grated mozzarella cheese
3 pepperoni slices

Supplies

Aluminum foil
Plastic knife
Measuring spoons

Recipe Directions

1. Place the muffin open-faced onto an aluminum foil square.
2. Spread the spaghetti sauce on the muffin.
3. Top with the pepperoni pieces. You may add other toppings at this point, if desired (mushrooms, onions, peppers).
4. Top the muffin pizza with cheese.
5. Bake for 15 minutes in a toaster oven or conventional oven at 375°F.
6. Let stand and cool before eating.

Nutty Banana Pop

Ingredients

1 banana
2 Tbsp. chopped peanuts
Chocolate candy coating

Supplies

Plastic bowl
Wax paper
Measuring spoons
Craft stick

Recipe Directions

1. Spread the chopped nuts on the wax paper.
2. Peel the banana and place on the stick.
3. Roll the banana in the nuts until entirely covered.
4. In the microwave, melt the chocolate candy coating.
5. Place the nutty banana in the coating mixture until covered.
6. Place the banana on the wax paper and freeze for 4 hours.
7. Eat and enjoy this nutty treat!

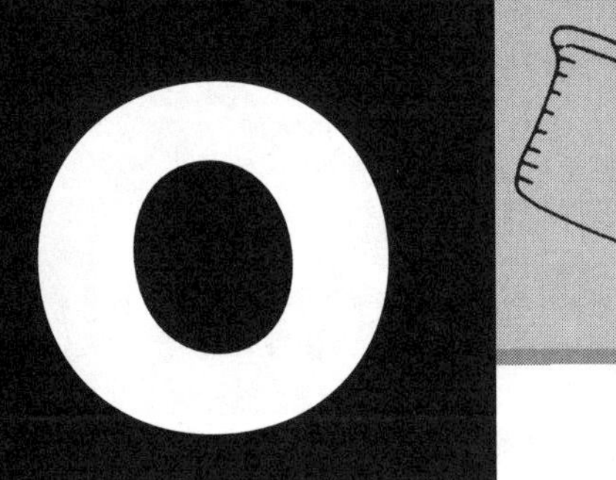

O. J. Plus

Ingredients

2 Tbsp. orange juice
2 Tbsp. plain yogurt
2 Tbsp. orange sherbet

Supplies

Measuring spoons
Blender
Plastic cup and straw

Recipe Directions

1. Measure the ingredients and place into the blender.
2. Mix on low for 1 minute or until the mixture is creamy and smooth.
3. Pour into a cup and enjoy!

Pudding Parfait

Ingredients

1 small sponge cake
$\frac{1}{2}$ cup of vanilla pudding
2 cups cold milk
2 Tbsp. of frozen strawberries (thawed)
3 Tbsp. whipped dairy topping

Supplies

Clear plastic cup
Plastic spoon and knife
Measuring spoons
Mixing bowl

Recipe Directions

1. Mix the pudding according to package directions.
2. Place half of the sponge cake in the bottom of the plastic cup.
3. Pour half of the pudding over the cake.
4. Top with half of the fruit topping.
5. Repeat the layering sequence.
6. Top with the remaining 1 Tbsp. of whipped dairy topping.

Quick-to-Fix Mix

Ingredients

1 Tbsp. toasted oat cereal
1 Tbsp. chocolate chips
1 Tbsp. chocolate coated candies
1 Tbsp. dry roasted peanuts
1 Tbsp. raisins
1 Tbsp. mini pretzels

Supplies

Plastic bowl
Measuring spoons
Plastic bag

Recipe Directions

1. Pour 1 Tbsp. of each ingredient into the plastic bag.
2. Shake the bag to mix the ingredients.
3. Place the mixed contents into the bowl.
4. Enjoy!

Rocky Road Sundae

Ingredients

$\frac{1}{2}$ cup chocolate ice cream
2 Tbsp. hot fudge topping
1 Tbsp. chopped almonds
2 Tbsp. marshmallows

Supplies

Measuring cup and spoons
Plastic spoon and bowl

Recipe Directions

1. Place the ice cream in a dish.
2. Melt the hot fudge topping and pour over the ice cream.
3. Top with marshmallows and chopped nuts.
4. Use your spoon to dig in and enjoy!

Sassy Salsa

Ingredients

$\frac{1}{4}$ cup salsa
1 Tbsp. yellow corn (drained)
1 Tbsp. black beans (drained)
2 Tbsp. crushed pineapple (not drained)
$\frac{1}{4}$ tsp. cilantro
Corn chips

Supplies

Measuring cups and spoons
Plastic bowl

Recipe Directions

1. Pour the salsa in the bowl.
2. Add beans, pineapple, and corn to the salsa.
3. Sprinkle with cilantro and mix.
4. Chill for 1 hour and serve with chips for dipping!

T

Terrific Tacos

Ingredients

$\frac{1}{4}$ lb. hamburger
1 mini taco shell
$\frac{1}{4}$ cup shredded lettuce
$\frac{1}{2}$ tomato, chopped
2 Tbsp. shredded cheese
1 Tbsp. chopped onions
$\frac{1}{2}$ tsp. taco seasoning
$\frac{1}{4}$ cup water

Supplies

Electric skillet or stove
Measuring cups and spoons
Paper plates

Recipe Directions

1. In the skillet, brown the hamburger and add seasoning and water.
2. Simmer this mixture on low for 10 minutes.
3. Chop the tomato into small pieces.
4. Measure the onions and cheese.
5. Place the meat inside the taco shell and add the tomato, cheese, and onions for delicious toppings.

The "Uncola®" Float

Ingredients

1 cup of clear cherry-flavored 7 UP®
$\frac{1}{2}$ cup vanilla ice cream
2 Tbsp. whipped dairy topping
1 red maraschino cherry

Supplies

Measuring spoons and cups
Plastic glass and spoon
Straw

Recipe Directions

1. Place the ice cream in a clear cup.
2. Pour the soda over the ice cream.
3. Top your float with whipped topping and a cherry.
4. Drink or eat this wonderful treat!

Vanishing Veggie Treat

Ingredients

1 crescent roll
2 oz. cream cheese
$\frac{1}{2}$ tsp. mayonnaise
$\frac{1}{3}$ tsp. sour cream
$\frac{1}{4}$ tsp. dill weed
1 sprinkle garlic salt
4 pieces of cauliflower
2 baby carrots (shredded)
4 pieces of broccoli
2 Tbsp. shredded cheddar cheese
Cooking spray

Supplies

Mixing bowl
Aluminum foil
Measuring cup and spoons
Plastic knife and fork

Recipe Directions

1. Spread the crescent roll onto a greased piece of aluminum foil and bake as directed on the package until golden brown.
2. While the crust is cooling, mix the cream cheese, mayonnaise, sour cream, dill weed, and garlic salt until creamy.
3. Chop the cauliflower and broccoli in small pieces.
4. Spread the mixture over the crust, and press the cut cauliflower and broccoli onto the mixture.
5. Sprinkle with carrots and cheese.
6. Chill completely before serving, and watch all those veggies vanish!

Wacky Wagon Wheels

Ingredients

$\frac{1}{2}$ celery stalk
1 Tbsp. peanut butter
4 carrot slices
8–10 raisins

Supplies

Toothpicks
Measuring spoons
Paper plates

Recipe Directions

1. Begin by inserting the toothpicks through the celery at the top and the bottom of the celery stalk.
2. Attach the four carrot coins (slices) on the sides of the celery as the wagon wheels.
3. Fill the celery with a peanut butter and raisin "cargo."
4. Load up and eat.

"X" Marks the Spot Biscuits

Ingredients

2 buttermilk refrigerator biscuits
1 Tbsp. butter (melted)
$\frac{1}{2}$ tsp. sugar
$\frac{1}{4}$ tsp. cinnamon
Cooking spray

Supplies

Measuring spoons
Aluminum foil
Cooking spray
Plastic spoons

Recipe Directions

1. Roll out each biscuit into a long tube shape.
2. Place the biscuits in a crisscross fashion in the shape of the letter X on a greased foil square.
3. Melt butter and mix with the cinnamon and sugar.
4. Spread this mixture on the biscuit and bake according to the package directions.
5. Let stand and cool for 10 minutes before eating.

Y

Yum Yum Dessert

Ingredients

$\frac{1}{4}$ angel food cake loaf
2 cups whipped dairy topping
$\frac{1}{4}$ cup marshmallows
$\frac{1}{4}$ cup frozen strawberries (thawed)

Supplies

Mixing bowl
Measuring cups and spoons
Plastic bowl

Recipe Directions

1. Tear up the angel food cake into small pieces.
2. In a mixing bowl, combine strawberries, topping, and marshmallows.
3. Fold in whipped topping mixture with the cake pieces until covered.
4. Chill until firm, and enjoy this yummy treat!

Z

Zesty Zucchini Pie

Ingredients

$\frac{1}{4}$ cup chopped zucchini
$\frac{1}{2}$ tomato, finely chopped
2 Tbsp. onions, finely chopped
3 Tbsp. Parmesan cheese
Cooking spray

Supplies

Muffin tins
Measuring cup and spoons
Plastic knife and spoon

Recipe Directions

1. Spray the muffin tin with cooking spray.
2. Place the biscuit in the tin, and bake according to the package directions.
3. Dice tomatoes, onions, and unpeeled zucchini.
4. Mix the chopped vegetables and cheese.
5. Place the mixed ingredients into the muffin cups.
6. Bake at 325°F for 25 minutes.
7. Cool and eat.

Recipe

Ingredients

Supplies

Recipe Directions

Rating the Recipe

Dear Families,

Please let me know how the cooking is going. All recipes get better as they are passed down from generation to generation, with each family adding its own special touches and secret ingredients. I would love to hear what you and your child thought of the cooking process. I will be sharing these reflections with other families, so your tips and advice will be appreciated.

Family name ______________________________

Recipe cooked ______________________________

The best part was ______________________________

____

____

____

Things I would change or add ______________________________

____

____

____

Additional thoughts ______________________________

____

____

____

Thanks for sharing!

Sincerely,

8 Why Workshop?

Parental participation in the literacy activities with their children can change the nature of interactions adults have with their child and serve as a catalyst for a variety of literacy learning opportunities. Based on the model that learning is social and interactive, the workshop approach is an effective way to continue your pathway toward partnership with families.

Just as your students learn by doing, parents in your classroom can benefit from this model as well. In a workshop approach, parents are actively involved throughout each session. The workshop time is a wonderful way for you to support families with learning initiatives and new ideas. This is also an important time for families as they form a network of support with other families as participants in the workshop. If the workshops continue, the relationship can flourish as families get more comfortable with you and one another.

Demonstration, discussion, and opportunities to reflect are key components of successful workshops. Workshop topics may range in type and purpose, but your goal remains the same: to seek ways of successfully involving parents that value their knowledge and expertise on their child. Workshops are a wonderful way to support parents and help them understand their important role as their child's first teacher.

Workshops are most successful when there is a balance of parent-teacher time as well as time to work with the students. Enlist your parents in brainstorming possible sessions and topics that could be addressed throughout the school year. The most powerful workshops are those based on the needs and concerns of families in your classroom. Sample workshop agendas and activities are included in this chapter to use as guides during your planning.

Getting Started

Now that you've decided to hold a workshop, there are a number of things you must do to plan for a successful experience. First, use the Workshop Presentation Planning Sheet on the next page as a way of organizing your thoughts and goals for the workshop.

Part of the planning process is deciding on a topic for your workshop. This chapter includes some sample workshop topics, along with tools for implementing them, starting on page 127.

After setting down your preliminary thoughts, it's a good idea to jot down an agenda for the workshop that is based on what you wrote on the planning sheet. Following is a sample agenda:

Sample Workshop Agenda

Opening/Ice Breaker
(10 minutes)

Introduction of the Featured Topic
(15 Minutes)

Hands-on Activity to involve parents in a project related to the topic
(30 minutes)

Sharing and Discussion
(15 minutes)

Closing and Wrap-up
(5 minutes)

Evaluation
(5 minutes)

This is a possible framework to follow and will be adjusted depending on the type and format of your workshop.

Workshop Presentation Planning Sheet

What major concepts do I want to stress in this presentation?

1. ______________________________

2. ______________________________

3. ______________________________

____

What would I like to achieve with participants as a result of this workshop?
What are the workshop goals?

____

____

____

Workshop goals for parents: ______________________________

students: ______________________________

myself: ______________________________

What resources are needed to make the workshop a success?

____

____

____

Are there resource people available with whom I might consult about this topic and/or invite to participate? Who are they and what can they contribute?

____

____

What are the plans for follow-up to this workshop?

____

____

How will I evaluate the success of the session? (survey, poll the parents, attitude)

____

____

Advertising the Workshop

You have done all the work, and the workshop is ready to go! Now it is time to let the parents know the when and where. Following is a list of suggestions to help in achieving a successful attendance rate. Keep in mind that attendance is an important goal, but only one aspect of parent involvement. We want parents to come to school, but it is not always possible to get every parent there. Be careful not to fall into the pattern of believing that only the parents who attend every scheduled event are the "good" ones and are more committed to helping their children. Many parents that cannot attend may have significant reasons for their absence. Continue to keep reaching out and encouraging all families to participate in any capacity that works for them.

Personal Invitation

The more personal, the better. Computer graphics are wonderful, but when the kids create and decorate, parents take notice. Invitations can also be sent from you, the principal, or another parent.

Telephone Calls

The telephone is a wonderful communication tool.

PHONE TREE

MARY	BETTY	LILA	DOUG
Thomas' 555-2120	Kramers 555-6866	Taylors 555-7268	Bennets 555-0253
Jenkins 555-1180	Honea's 555-1150	Smiths 555-5885	Rizzo's 555-6661
Diazo's 555-1140	Frazee's 555-3661	Bianco's 555-6988	Longs 555-6053

1. Set up a phone tree and have parents in charge of "spreading the word."

2. Reminder calls 24 hours before the event are helpful for busy parents.

3. Leave messages on voice mail or answering machines.

Banners or Flyers

Students can create banners or flyers to let their parents know when and where a special event will take place. (Messages can also be placed on the school sign, if possible.) Be sure to include messages stating why you need them there. For example:

Please join us for our

Family Reading Night

Time: 8:00–9:00
Place: School Cafeteria
Date: October 14

Remember:

Better schools begin with your involvement. We will see you then!

Community Sites

Place signs and flyers at the local stores and businesses where parents go when they are not at school. If it is not possible for parents to drop off or pick up their child at school, they still can have access to the information. Ask the neighborhood grocer, church, community center, bowling alley, gas station, or business for permission. Most of these agencies love to support the schools in an effort to involve the community and families.

If it is a large school event, you may want to check out advertising on the local radio station, newspaper, or TV.

Whatever the event, try to use multiple modes of communication. Send out letters and invitations, and then follow-up with phone calls or a personal contact. The more times and ways that parents can get the message that teachers do want them there, and that teachers do need their involvement, the more successful teachers will be at achieving their goals.

The Workshop Day Arrives

In his book *Life in a Crowded Place* (1992), Ralph Peterson stated the most important thing he had learned about teaching was that

> *Community in itself is more important to learning than any method or technique. Learning has to do with our desire to make sense of our experience, to join with others, to become a part of a community. . . . We as educators need to extend community beyond the classroom walls.*

For your parent workshops to be most successful, this community spirit must prevail among the family participants. Your first goal must be for parents and family members to attain a comfort level that will promote the sharing and exchanging of ideas. Parents are people first, and people need to get to know one another if they are expected to work together in a collaborative fashion. First, have all parents sign in on the sheet provided on page 126. Then, once everyone is seated and you have their attention, it is time to put parents at ease.

Here are a few getting-to-know-you questions that might help you.

1. Share one news item from your week: a "high"; a "low."
2. Describe the teacher that you remember most fondly. What stands out in your mind?
3. Share the thing you do to relax each week.
4. What is your favorite story or book? Why is it so special?
5. What book does your child want you to read over and over?
6. Share your most unique talent.
7. What was your best/worst learning experience?
8. Choose a breakfast cereal that best represents your personality.
9. Share the compliment that you receive most often.
10. Choose something from your wallet or bag that represents you in some way.

You will know your audience's comfort level best. Use your imagination and create new icebreakers. If you are doing several workshops consecutively, give the participants the job of creating a question, and see what they come up with.

Workshop Sign-In Sheet

Topic: ______________________________ Date: ______________

Parent Name:

____

____

____

____

____

____

____

____

____

____

____

____

____

____

____

____

____

____

____

____

____

____

Sample Workshop Ideas

Family Time Capsule

Preserve family memories by helping families organize and fill a time capsule. Time capsules have always been a way to pass personal artifacts to future generations. The idea of filling a container with memories has a special appeal knowing that you are forging a link with future generations by assembling treasures to be opened at a later time. This activity can be initiated at every grade level and requires a minimum of materials.

1. Share the letter on page 128 with families, inviting them to collect artifacts and special mementos to bring and share with other families at school.
2. Brainstorm with students and family members what type of objects would best represent each family member.
3. Block out at least 1 hour of time for parents to sort through, discuss, and narrow down the items they most want to enclose in the capsule.
4. Have parents and students decorate the outer layer of the capsule and decide a place for the capsule to be stored and the date for the retrieval of this precious treasure.
5. Have families create a list to document its contents as well as where the capsule will be stored.
6. Celebrate and have the group share the decorated and filled capsules over some cookies and juice.

Here are some tips for holding a successful time capsule workshop.

1. If families are still finding it hard to collect items, offer them these additional suggestions:
   - *Notes, letters, or stories from extended family members*
   - *A picture or drawing representing their child's favorite book*
   - *Family journal pages*
   - *Any school work sample to show their child's academic growth*
   - *Family recipes*
   - *Stamps or buttons to commemorate the time*
   - *Article of popular clothing*
   - *Favorite children's book or toys*
2. You have several options for a time capsule container. Capsules are available to purchase and range in price from $20 to $50. If you are going for durability, aluminum and stainless steel containers work well. Use a strong, waterproof enclosure that can be sealed tightly to keep out water and air.
3. Encourage parents not to bury the capsule, but rather to store their capsule in a cool, dry place, such as a closet. The attic may keep in heat and humidity, which will damage the contents.
4. Family time capsules can be officially registered with the International Time Capsule Society at www.oglethorpe.edu/itcs or at The International Time Capsule Society, Oglethorpe University, 4484 Peachtree Road NE, Atlanta, GA 300319-2797.
5. Provide markers, stickers, painting, pens, or paint for families to decorate and document both the inside and outside of this treasure.

Time Capsule Workshop

Dear Families,

I would like to invite you to come to school on ___________________ to create and fill a family time capsule. A time capsule can be a wonderful project, a time for everyone to get together and collect memorabilia, stories, and special items and photos. I would like you to take some time looking around and collecting what you think might be important representations of memories to preserve. Here are some possibilities to consider:

Photographs: These are one of the best ways to document your family, events, pets, and favorite things. Be sure to list people and events with full names and dates.

Your child's work: The time capsule can become a profile for your child's growth and development. You can "dig" up pictures drawn years ago, samples of your child's writing, and special projects on which they have worked hard.

Letters: Love expressed through writing transcends time. There is nothing that can stir up special memories more than reading a past birthday card or special note sent to one another. Another idea is to write your own messages to your child, describing memorable moments in his or her life.

Newspapers: What is in the news today can be interesting conversation in years to come. Special editions are a nice way to record current historical events. You may want to include the entire paper of a special date or just include sections.

Miscellaneous: There is no correct way to fill a time capsule. It is a representation of your family the way you can say it best. Other ideas might include: vacation highlights, tickets, magazines, menus to your favorite family restaurant, special shared secrets or memories, and, of course, your child's favorite book and story. As much time and thought should go into selecting the items as to selecting the time capsule itself. Enjoy the search, and I will see you on the ___________________.

Sincerely,

Poetry Workshop

This is a great way to share how powerful poetry can be for both children and adults. Here is a simple biographical poem format that parents can use to write about their child.

Bio-Poem

Line 1	Child's First Name
Line 2	Something they do outside school
Line 3	Four words to describe your child
Line 4	Lover of . . . (3 things or ideas)
Line 5	Who believes (1 or more ideas)
Line 6	Who wants (3 things)
Line 7	Who uses (3 methods of things)
Line 8	Who gives (3 things)
Line 9	Who says (A quote)
Line 10	Last name

You may create your own personal version of the bio-poem or use the one we have included to model what the final version looks like. Each family can share their finished poems. Students can create an illustration to display next to the poetry in your classrooms. These poems can become special keepsakes for the parents and the students. Following is one example of a biopoem.

Ryan

Rider of bikes and climber of trees

Loveable, inquisitive, vibrant, energetic

Lover of family, play, and books

Who believes he can do anything

Who wants his mommy and daddy

Who uses toys, books, and his big brown eyes

Who gives great hugs and kisses

Who says, "I am special!"

Maiers

Our Family Workshop

This workshop can be done at school or you can send instructions home with family members to complete. After the project is completed, it is suggested that each child or family can share its poster.

Goal: *For each family to recognize their unique and special qualities*

Materials

Materials needed for each participant:

One large sheet of posterboard (cardboard will also work)

Markers

Computer labels

Family pictures or magazines

Glue or rubber cement

Procedure

1. Have each family member look through old pictures or magazines to find snapshots of activities they enjoy doing together, favorite foods, special toys, books, sports, pets, or past vacation spots.
2. Arrange the pictures on the posterboard, and have each family member write captions under the photographs to describe the object or events depicted in the photos. For example:

   A doll is Abby's favorite toy.

   Skiing is our favorite family sport.

   Mom cooks the best apple pie!
3. You may want to supply yarn, paint, glitter, or other materials to put the special finishing touches on the poster.
4. A wonderful culmination of this activity is a brief "Family Life Story" presentation. Each family could present their family poster and share parts of their story with other families. This is a great community-building activity for long-term family work. Having the parents stay and enjoy coffee and some cookies following the presentations really provides some "connecting" and community time.

The Marvelous Memory Jar

This workshop can help families create a wonderful gift to give to someone special in a child's life or used as a special keepsake of times shared as a family. When planning this workshop, send the letter on page 132 to parents. The letter explains the purpose of the jar. When families have chosen a jar, invite them in to design, decorate, and share their jars.

The Very Good Yearbook Workshop

Set aside an evening for families to come together to create a yearbook. Send the letter on page 133 to parents. Then supply families with a three-ring binder with several blank pages. With their child, families can organize and decorate their family albums. Leave some blank pages to add on as the year progresses.

Read-Aloud Workshop

Invite families to come to school at a convenient time to share their tips on reading to their child. Use the handout on page 134 as a guide to talk to families about the importance of reading to their children.

On the day of the workshop, model for parents by reading aloud your favorite story or picture book. Show how you use expression. Ask questions, and celebrate students' responses. Provide books from your school library or personal collection for parents to use in practicing these strategies with their child.

After this interactive session with families, have materials available, such as colored paper, pencils, markers, books of paper, and stamps, for families to use to respond to the books. Share and celebrate the responses.

After It's Over

It is important when you meet with families that you give them the opportunity to share their feedback confidentially. This will ensure that you are meeting their needs as you plan for future contacts. On page 135 is a sample workshop evaluation form that you can use as is or adapt to your topic and needs.

Marvelous Memory Jar Workshop

Dear Families:

I would like to invite you to come to school on__________to create and fill a marvelous memory jar. To create a memory jar, follow these instructions. Hope to see you at the workshop!

1. Begin by choosing a family member or friend for whom you and your child would like to do something special. It could be dad, grandmother, grandfather, aunt, or uncle. Talk with your child about to whom he or she will give this special gift.
2. Find a unique jar, one with a shape or design that really stands out. Have your child help you pick out the jar.
3. You and your child should bring your jar to the workshop, where you and your child can decorate the jar with watercolors, puffy paint, or markers. You may want to add other special touches, such as yarn, ribbon, or sequins.
4. Each time your child spends time with the recipient, help them take a few moments to dictate and write down what they did together. This can be a special occasion or just a memory of the little things that are done every day. Here are some examples:

   Dear Dad: Thanks for taking me fishing.

   Dear Grandmother: I remember when you told me the story of your mother.

   Dear Uncle Mark: I remember when you showed me your stamp collection.

   Dear Mom: I love the story you read me every night.

   Dear Grandpa: Thank you for making me feel better when I was sick.
5. Set time aside each week to sit down with your child to talk about these memories. You may want to have the paper already cut into strips so that you can quickly jot ideas down. You may do the writing as your child tells you the story, or you may let your child put his or her own thoughts in writing. It would be fun to do a little of both.
6. Collect and record these memories over a few months or even the year.
7. Pick a special holiday, birthday, or occasion to present this rare treasure to the beloved person. Be sure to send instructions for them to choose a memory to read each day or when they are feeling down. Wait until you see the reaction!

Sincerely,

The Very Good Yearbook Workshop

Dear Families,

Please join us at school to create this simple project full of fun and memories. Help your child transform a three-ring notebook into a year of memories and milestones. All you need to begin is a three-ring binder and some imagination. I supply the binder and you supply the imagination!

Here are some ideas to help you get started thinking. Bring your ideas and samples of the following:

- Favorite photos
- "Things That We Did" over the year
- School subject your child loved
- Teacher's name
- Best friends
- Favorite songs
- What I am proudest of . . .
- Favorite clothes
- Special foods
- A self-portrait
- Vacation highlights
- Birthday cards
- Sports I love to play or watch
- My first/last day of school
- Summer (draw or write)
- Most/least

You may also want to interview your child and record his or her hopes, dreams, and goals for the coming year. This can be an ongoing way to connect with your child. It will be a treasured prize for years to come.

Helpful Hint: *You may want to purchase tabs to divide the pages for the designated years.*

Sincerely,

Reading Aloud

Reading aloud helps your child to

Enjoy reading
Build vocabulary
Predict
Develop story sense
Understand language and literacy
Listen better
Read more!

Parents are the most powerful models for demonstrating the power and value of reading!

Workshop Evaluation

Dear Families,

Now that today's workshop is over, I would like to know how you feel and what you think about the things we did so I can continually make our time together better and more productive. Your opinion is very important to me, so please take a few moments to answer the following questions honestly. Your answers will remain confidential.

Workshop Content or Topic ______________________________

Time and Date ______________________________

1. What did you enjoy most about today/tonight?

____

____

2. Please share what you found most helpful.

____

____

3. Did the workshop meet your expectations? Please share.

____

____

4. What would you do differently? Suggestions or comments:

____

____

5. Your overall rating of today's project.

1 (best) 2 3 4 (least) 5

Thank you for sharing your thoughts.

Sincerely,

Appendix

Resources

Books and Pamphlets

Partnerships and Parent Involvement Program Profiles

Ban, J., *Parents Assuring Student Success (PASS)*, 1993. National Education Service, 1252 Loesch Road, P.O. Box 8, Station T6, Bloomington, IN 47402-0008, 812-336-7701.

Building Capacity for Partnership Through Networking, Claud E. Leiby, Region IV Supervisor, Title 1 School Districts of Southwest Florida, 3135 North Washington Boulevard, Sarasota, FL 34234-6299, 941-359-5650.

"Creating Healthy Communities," Source, August 1996, pp. 1-3. 800-888-7828.

Information for Building Partnerships

Epstein, J. L., *School/Family/Community Partnerships: Caring for the Children We Share*, 1995.

Epstein, J. L., Coates, INITIALS?, Salinas, K. C., & Simon, B. S., *School, Family, and Community Partnerships: Your Handbook for Action*, 1997.

Baghban, M., *How Can I Help My Child Learn to Read English as a Second Language?*, 1970.

Chan, J. M. T., *Why Read Aloud to Children?*, 1974.

Eberly, D., *How Does My Child's Vision Affect His Reading?*, 1970.

Glazer, S. M., *How Can I Help My Child Build Positive Attitudes Toward Reading?*, 1980.

Rogers, N., *How Can I Help My Child Get Ready to Read?*, YEAR?.

General Resources

Adams, M., *Beginning to Read: Thinking and Learning About Print.* Cambridge, MA: The MIT Press, 1994.

Ainsworth, R. G., *Turning Potential School Dropouts into Graduates: The Case for School-based One-on-One Tutoring.* Washington, DC: National Commission for Employment Policy, 1995.

Arnold, C., *Read with Me: A Guide for Student Volunteers Starting Early Childhood Literacy Programs.* Washington, DC: U.S. Department of Education, Office of Educational Research and Improvement, 1997.

Berger, E., *Parents as Partners in Education: Families and Schools Working Together.* Columbus, OH: Prentice Hall, 1994.

Blevins, W., *Phonics from A to Z: A Proactive Guide.* New York: Scholastic, 1998.

Bloom, B., *Developing Talent in Young People.* New York: Ballantine, 1985.

Brachman-Buzzell, J., *School and Family Partnerships: Case Studies for Regular and Special Educators.* Albany, NY: Delmar Publishers, 1996.

Braunger, J., & Lewis, J. P., *Building a Knowledge Base in Reading.* Portland, OR: Northwest Regional Educational Laboratory, 1997.

Building School-Family Partnerships for Learning: Workshops for Urban Educators. Washington, DC: U.S. Department of Education, 1995.

Cambourne, B., *The Whole Story: Natural Learning and the Acquisition of Literacy in the Classroom.* New York: Scholastic, 1998.

Carrasquillo, A., & London, C. B. G., *Parents and Schools: A Source Book, Volume 775.* Hamden, CT: Garland Reference Library of Social Science, 1993.

Center for the Improvement of Early Reading Achievement, *Every Child a Reader.* Ann Arbor, MI: University of Michigan, 1998.

Chall, J., *Stages of Reading Development.* Orlando, FL: Harcourt Brace, 1996.

Chall, J., & Curtis, M., *Diagnostic Achievement Testing in Reading.* New York: Guilford Press, 1990.

Chall, J., Roswell, F., Fletcher, M., & Richard, D., *Teaching Children to Read: A Step-by-Step Guide for Volunteer Tutors.* Elizabethtown, PA: Continental Press, 1998.

Cheatham, J. B., *Help a Child Learn to Read.* Syracuse, NY: Literacy Volunteers of America, 1998.

Clay, M., *The Early Detection of Reading Difficulties.* Portsmouth, NH: Heinemann, 1996.

Clay, M., *Becoming Literate.* Portsmouth, NH: Heinemann, 1991.

Collins, R., *Reading Helpers: A Handbook for Training Tutors.* Vienna, VA: Collins Management Consulting, 1998.

Collins, S., *Our Children Are Watching: Ten Skills for Leading the Next Generation to Success.* Barrytown: Barrytown Ltd., 1995.

Cooper, J., Pikulski, J., & Au, K., *Early Success: An Intervention Program.* Boston: Houghton Mifflin, 1996.

Cullinan, B. E., *Read to Me: Raising Kids Who Love to Read.* New York: Scholastic, 1992.

Cunningham, P., *Phonics They Use: Words for Reading and Writing.* New York: HarperCollins, 1995.

Cunningham P., & Hall, D., *Making Words.* Carthage, IL: Good Apple, 1994.

Davis, D., & Lewis, J. P., *Tips for Parents About Reading.* Portland, OR: Northwest Regional Educational Laboratory, 1997.

Dedford, D. E., Lyons, C. A., & Pinnell, G. S., *Bridges to Literacy.* Portsmouth, NH: Heinemann, 1991.

Diss, R. E., *Recruiting and Training Volunteer Tutors of Emergent and Beginning Readers in the Primary Grades.* Arlington, VA: Appalachian Educational Laboratory, 1998.

Faber, A., Mazlish, E., Nyberg, L., & Templeton, R., *How to Talk So Kids Can Learn: At Home and in School.* New York: Fireside Press, 1996.

Farkas, G., Warren, M., & Johnson, A., *Reading One-to-One: The UTD Structures Tutoring Program Manual.* Dallas, TX: Center for Education and Social Sciences, University of Texas at Dallas, 1998.

Flansburg, S., *Math Magic for Your Kids.* New York: William Morrow, 1997.

Fountas, I. C., & Pinnell, G. S., *Guided Reading: Good First Teaching for All Children.* Portsmouth, NH: Heinemann, 1996.

Fountas, I. C., & Pinnell, G. S., *Training Kit for Literacy Volunteers.* Portsmouth, NH: Heinemann, 1998.

Frutcher, N., Galletta, A., & White, J. L., New *Directions in Parent Involvement.* New York: Academy for Educational Development, 1992.

Fry, E. B., Fountoukidis, D. L., & Polk, J. K., *The New Reading Teacher's Book of Lists.* Englewood Cliffs, NJ: Prentice Hall, 1984.

Gesell, A., Frances, I., & Ames, L. B., *The Child from Five to Ten.* New York: Harper & Row, 1977.

Guthrie, J., & Wigfield, A., *Reading Engagement: Motivating Readers Through Integrated Instruction.* Newark, DE: International Reading Association, 1995.

Henderson, A. C., *The Evidence Continues to Grow: Parent Involvement Improves Student Achievement.* Columbia, MD: National Committee for Citizens in Education, 1987.

Hamilton, L., *Child's Play 6-12: 160 Instant Activities, Crafts, and Science Projects for Grade Schoolers.* New York: Three Rivers Press, 1997.

Hermann, B., Handbook for Tutor Volunteers. Newark, DE: International Reading Association, 1995.

Hiebert, E. H., & Taylor, B. M., *Getting Reading Right from the Start: Effective Early Literacy Interventions.* Boston: Allyn and Bacon, 1994.

Houston, M., *Reading Coaches: Basic Training.* Franklin, KY: Reading Coaches, 1997.

Houston, M., *Reading Coaches: Facilitator's Manual.* Franklin, KY: Reading Coaches, 1998.

Houston, M., *Reading Coaches: Word Exploration Activities.* Franklin, KY: Reading Coaches, 1998.

Internizzi, M., Meier, J. D., Swank, L., & Juel, C., *Phonological Awareness Literacy Screening.* Charlottesville, VA: University Printing, 1998.

Johns, J., *Basic Reading Inventory.* Dubuque, IA: Kendall-Hunt, 1997.

Johnston, F., Invernizzi, M., & Juel, C., *Book Buddies: Guidelines for Volunteer Tutors of Emergent and Early Readers.* New York: Guilford Press, 1998.

Kameenui, E., & Simmons, D., *America Reads Challenge: Read*Write*Now.* Washington, DC: Blue Sky Press, 1996.

Kelly, M., *The Mother's Almanac II: Your Child from Six to Twelve.* New York: Doubleday, 1989.

Korlek, D., & Collins R., *On the Road to Reading: A Guide for Community Partners.* Vienna, VA: Collins Management Consulting, 1997.

Levesque, J., *Missouri-Reads: A Pilot Guide for Tutors.* St. Louis, MO: LIFT-Missouri, 1998.

Levine, J., *Getting Men Involved: Strategies for Early Childhood Programs.* New York: Families and Work Institute, 1993.

Lipson, M. Y., & Wixson, K. K., *Assessment and Instruction of Reading and Writing Disability.* New York: Longman, 1997.

MacDonald, R. B., *The Master Tutor: A Guidebook for More Effective Tutoring.* Williamsville, NY: Cambridge Stratford, 1996.

MacDonald, R. B., *Tutor Evaluation and Self-Assessment Tool.* Williamsville, NY: Cambridge Stratford, 1996.

McGee L., & Richgels, J., *Literacy's Beginnings: Supporting Young Readers and Writers.* Boston: Allyn and Bacon, 1996.

McGlip, J., & Michael, M., *The Home-School Connection.* Portsmouth, NH: Heinemann, 1994.

Mack, A., *A+ Parents: Help Your Child Learn and Succeed in School.* Ithaca, NY: McBooks Press, 1997.

Maiers, A., & Nistler, R.J., *Changing Parent Roles in School: Effects of a School-Based Family Literacy Program in an Urban First-Grade Classroom.* In T. Shanahan and F. V. Rodriguez-Brown, eds., National Reading Conference Yearbook 47 (pp. 221–32). Austin, TX: National Reading Conference, 1997.

Maiers, A., & Nistler, R. J., Stopping the Silence: Hearing Parent Voices in an Urban First-Grade Family Literacy Program. *The Reading Teacher* 53(8): 670–80.

Maiers, A., & Nistler, R. J., Exploring Home-School Connections: A Family Literacy Perspective on Improving Urban Schools. *Education and Urban Society* 32(1):3-17.

Mooney, M., *Developing Life-long Readers.* Wellington, New Zealand: Learning Media, 1988.

Mooney, M., *Reading to, with, and by Children.* Katonah, NY: Richard C. Owen Press, 1990.

Morris, D., *Case Studies in Teaching Beginning Readers: The Howard Street Tutoring Manual.* Boone, NC: Fieldstream, 1992.

Morrow, L., & Walker, B., *A Handbook for Volunteer Tutors K-3.* Newark, DE: International Reading Association, 1997.

Mostafa, M., *Beyond Traditional Phonics: Research Discoveries and Reading Instruction.* Portsmouth, NH: Heinemann, 1997.

Opitz, M., *Flexible Grouping in Reading: Practical Ways to Help All Students Become Better Readers.* New York: Scholastic, 1998.

Ostrow, J., *A Room with a Different View: First Through Third Graders Build Community and Create Curriculum.* York, ME: Stenhouse, 1995.

Papert, S., *The Connected Family: Bridging the Digital Generation Gap.* Marietta, GA: Longstreet, 1996.

Peterson, R., *Life in a Crowded Place: Making a Learning Community.* Portsmouth, NH: Heinemann, 1992.

Pinnell, G. S., & Fountas, I. C., *Help America Read: A Handbook for Volunteers.* Portsmouth, NH: Heinemann, 1997.

Power, B. M., & Hubbard, R., *Literacy in Process: The Heinemann Reader.* Portsmouth, NH: Heinemann, 1991.

Raines, S. & Canady, R., *Story Stretchers for the Primary Grades: Activities to Expand Children's Favorite Books.* Mt. Ranier, MD: Gryphon House, 1992.

Ramsey, D. L., *Motivation.* Emerson, NY: Performance Learning Systems, 1990.

Reaching All Families: Creating Family-Friendly Schools. Washington, DC: U.S. Department of Education, 1996.

Rich, D., *MegaSkills: How Families Can Help Children Succeed in School and Beyond.* Boston: Houghton Mifflin, 1988.

Rioux, J. W., & Berla, N., *Innovations in Parent and Family Involvement.* Princeton, NJ: Eye on Education, 1993.

Rogers, M., *Planning for Title I Programs: Guidelines for Parents, Advocates, and Educators.* Washington, DC: Center for Law and Education, 1995.

Roller, C., *So . . . What's a Tutor to Do?* Newark, DE: International Reading Association, 1998.

Roller, C., *Variability not Disability: Struggling Readers in the Workshop Classroom.* Newark, DE: International Reading Association, 1996.

Rosenthal, N. *Teach Someone to Read: A Step-by-Step Guide for Literacy Tutors.* Belmont, CA: Fearon/Janus/Quercus, 1998.

Routman, R., *Invitations: Changing as Teachers and Learners.* Portsmouth, NH: Heinemann, 1994.

Saphire, J., & Gower, R., *The Skillful Teacher: Building Your Teaching Skills.* Carlisle, MA: Research for Better Teaching, 1997.

Shockley, B., Michalove, B., & Allen, J., *Engaging Families.* Portsmouth, NH: Heinemann, 1995.

Silberstein-Storfer, M., *Doing Art Together: Discovering the Joys of Appreciating and Creating as Taught at the Metropolitan Museum of Art's Famous Parent-Child Workshop.* New York: Harry N. Abrams, 1997.

Stribling, A., *50 Simple Things You Can Do to Raise a Child Who Loves History and Geography.* New York: Arco, 1997.

Snow, C. E., Burns, M. S., & Griffin, P., *Preventing Reading Difficulties in Young Children.* Washington, DC: National Academy Press, 1998.

Sobol, T., & Sobol, H., *Your Child in School.* New York: Arbor House, 1987.

SotoMayor, M., *Empowering Hispanic Families: A Critical Issue for the 90's.* Milwaukee, WI: Family Service America, 1991.

Starting Points. New York: Carnegie Corporation of New York, 1994.

Strong Families, Strong Schools: Building Community Partnerships for Learning. Washington, DC: U.S. Department of Education, 1994.

Taylor, D., *Many Families, Many Literacies.* Portsmouth, NH: Heinemann, 1997.

Taylor, D., & Dorsey-Gaines, C., *Growing Up Literate: Learning From Inner-City Families.* Portsmouth, NH: Heinemann, 1998.

Trelease, J., *The New Read-Aloud Handbook.* New York: Penguin Books, 1989.

Trelease, J., *The Read-Aloud Handbook.* New York: Penguin Books, 1982.

21st Learning Challenge Volunteer Resource Manual. Rochester, NY: Eastman Kodak Company, 1995.

Vades, G., *Con Respeto: Bridging the Distance Between Culturally Diverse Families and the Schools.* Williston, VT: Teacher's College Press, 1996.

Vopat, J., *More Than Bake Sales.* York, ME: Stenhouse, 1998.

Vopat, J., *The Parent Project.* York, ME: Stenhouse, 1996.

Weaver, C., Gillmeister-Krause, L., & Vento-Zogby, G., *Creating Support for Effective Literacy Instruction.* Portsmouth, NH: Heinemann, 1996.

Zahler, K. *50 Simple Things That You Can Do to Raise a Child Who Loves Math.* New York: Macmillan General Reference, 1997.

Government Agencies

Head Start
U.S. Department of Health and Human Services
Administration for Children and Families
Office of Public Affairs
370 L'Enfant Promenade, SW
Washington, DC 20202
202-205-8572

Office of Educational Research and Improvement
U.S. Department of Education
555 New Jersey Avenue, NW
Washington, DC 20208
202-219-1935

Parent Training and Information Systems Program
Office of Special Education Programs
U.S. Department of Education
600 Independence Avenue, SW
Switzer Building, Room 4613
Washington, DC 20202
202-205-5507

Title I and Even Start
U.S. Department of Education
Compensatory Education Programs
Office of Elementary and Secondary Education
600 Independence Avenue, SW
Room 4400, Portals Building
Washington, DC 20202-6132
202-260-0826

Journals

Educational Leadership
Association for Supervision and Curriculum Development
1250 North Pitt Street
Alexandria, VA 22314-1453

Language Arts
National Council of Teachers of English
1111 West Kenyon Road
Urbana, IL 61801-1096

Making the Connection, A Weekly Report from Education Week
4301 Connecticut Avenue, NW, Suite 250
Washington, DC 20008

Phi Delta Kappan
Phi Delta Kappa, Inc.
408 North Union
P.O. Box 789
Bloomington, IN 47402

Primary Voices, K-6
National Council of Teachers of English
1111 West Kenyon Road
Urbana, IL 61801-1096

The Reading Teacher
International Reading Association
800 Barksdale Road
P.O. Box 8139
Newark, DE 19714-8139

Organizations

Alliance for Parental Involvement in Education
P.O. Box 59
East Chatham, NY 12060-0059

American Library Association
50 East Huron Street
Chicago, IL 60611

ASPIRA Association, Inc.
Parent Leadership Programs
1444 Eye Street NW, Suite 800
Washington, DC 20005

Black Hills Parent Resource Network
Black Hills Special Services Foundation
P.O. Box 218
Sturgis, SD 57785

Building Family Strengths
Parent Information Center
P.O. Box 2405
Concord, NH 03302-2405

Center for Healthy Families
Sunrise Children's Hospital Foundation
3196 South Maryland Parkway, 307
Las Vegas, NV 89109

Center for Social Organization of Schools
Johns Hopkins University
3505 North Charles Street
Baltimore, MD 21218

Center on Families, Communities, Schools, and Children's Learning
Publications Department
Center on School, Family, and Community Partnerships
Johns Hopkins University
3505 North Charles Street
Baltimore, MD 21218

Center on Fathers, Families, and Public Policy
Family Resource Center
200 South Michigan Avenue
Chicago, IL 60601

Children's Home Society of Washington
201 South 34th Street
Tacoma, WA 98408

Clearinghouse for Immigrant Education (CHIME)
National Coalition for Advocates for Students
100 Boylston Street, Suite 737
Boston, MA 02116

Colorado Parent Information and Resource Center
Clayton Foundation
1445 Market Street, Suite 350
Denver, CO 80202

Connections
Geneseo Migrant Center, Inc.
P.O. Box 545
Geneseo, NY 14454

Corporation for National Service
1201 New York Avenue, NW
Washington, DC 20525

Dad to Dad
3771 Admiral Drive
Atlanta, GA 30341

Families Resource Coalition
200 South Michigan Avenue, Suite 1520
Chicago, IL 60604

The Fatherhood Project
Families and Work Institute
330 Seventh Avenue, 14th Floor
New York, NY 10001

Fathers' Resource Center
Loring Park Office Building
430 Oak Grove Street, Suite 105
Minneapolis, MN 55403

Florida Center for Parent Involvement
Center of Excellence
7406 North Dixon Avenue
Tampa, FL 33604

Families and Schools Together (FAST)
Pacer Center, Inc.
4826 Chicago Avenue South
Minneapolis, MN 55417-1098

Families United for Success
Life Services Systems for Communities and Schools
272 East 8th Street, Suite B
Holland, MI 49423

Family Focus Project
Mental Health Association of Texas
8401 Shoal Creek Blvd.
Austin, TX 78757

Family Resource Project
Maine Parent Federation, Inc.
P.O. Box 2067
Augusta, ME 04338-2067

Greater Washington Urban League
3501 14th Street, NW
Washington, DC 20010

Hispanic Policy Development Project
1001 Connecticut Avenue, NW
Washington, DC 20036

The Home and School Institute
1201 16th Street, NW
Washington, DC 20036

Institute for Responsive Education
704 Commonwealth Avenue
Boston, MA 02215

International Reading Association
800 Barksdale Road
P.O. Box 8139
Newark, DE 19714-8139

Iowa Parent Resource Center
The Higher Plain, Inc.
1025 Penkridge Drive
Iowa City, IA 52246

Learning Disabilities Association of America
4156 Library Road
Pittsburgh, PA 15234

Massachusetts Parent Training and Empowerment Project
Cambridge Partnership for Public Education
MIT Building 20, Room 129B
77 Massachusetts Avenue
Cambridge, MA 02139

Mexican American Legal Defense and Education Fund
634 South Spring Street, 11th Floor
Los Angeles, CA 90014

Missouri Partnership for Parenting Assistance
Literacy Investment for Tomorrow (LIFT)
300 South Broadway
St. Louis, MO 63102

National Association for Education of Young Children
1509 16th Street, NW
Washington, DC 20036-1426

National Center for Fathering
10200 West 75th Street, Suite 267
Shawnee Mission, KS 66204-2223

National Center on Fathers & Families
Graduate School of Education
University of Pennsylvania
Philadelphia, PA 19104

National Center for Family Literacy
Waterfront Plaza, Suite 200
325 West Main Street
Louisville, KY 40202-4251

National Coalition for Parent Involvement in Education
Box 39
1201 16th Street, NW
Washington, DC 20002

National Committee for Citizens in Education
10840 Little Patuxent Parkway, 301
Columbia, MD 21044-3199

National Congress of Parent Teacher Associations
700 Rush Street
Chicago, IL 60711

National Council for Family Relations
3989 Central, NE
Suite 550
Minneapolis, MN 55421

National Institute for Literacy
800 Connecticut Avenue, NW
Suite 200
Washington, DC 71309-1230

National Parenting Association
65 Central Park West, Suite 1D
New York, NY 10023

Native American Parental Assistance Program
Ahmium Education, Inc.
P.O. Box 366
San Jacinto, CA 92581

Northwest Regional Educational Laboratory
101 SW Main Street, Suite 500
Portland, OR 97204-3212

Ohio Parent Information Resource Center
Lighthouse Youth Services, Inc.
4837 Ward Street
Cincinnati, OH 45227

Parent Partner
Exceptional Children's Assistance Center
P.O. Box 16
Davidson, NC 28036

Parent Training Resource Assistance Center
Community Partnership for Education
901 North Jackson Street
Albany, GA 31702-1726

Parental Assistance Centers
Parents and Children Together
1475 Linapuni Street, Room 117-A
Honolulu, HI 96818

Parental Assistance Program
Licking Valley Community Action Program
203 High Street
Flemingsburg, KY 41041

Parenting Resource and Support Partnership
Childcare Connection, Inc.
332 W. Edmondson Drive
Rockville, MD 20852

Parents as Partner
1401 NE 70th Street
Oklahoma City, OK 73111

Parents First
NashvilleREAD, Inc.
421 Great Circle Road, Suite 104
Nashville, TN 37228

National Black Child Development Institute
1023 15th Avenue, NW
Suite 600
Washington, DC 20002

Parents in Touch
Indianapolis Public Schools
901 North Carrollton
Indianapolis, IN 46202

Parents Plus of Wisconsin
P.O. Box 452
328 Sixth Street
Menasha, WI 54952-0452

Prevent Child Abuse
New Jersey Chapter, Inc.
35 Halsey Street, Suite 300
Newark, NJ 07102-3031

Reading Is Fundamental
Smithsonian Institution
600 Maryland Avenue, SW
Suite 600
Washington, DC 20024-2540

Southwestern Pennsylvania Parental Assistance Center Project
Community Action Southwest
22 West High Street
Waynesburg, PA 15370

Vermont Family Resource Partnership
Addison County Parent Child Center
P.O. Box 646
Middlebury, VT 05753

Television

ABC Community Relations
ABC-TV
1330 Avenue of the Americas
New York, NY 10019-5402

CBS Television Reading Program
51 West 52nd Street
New York, NY 10018-6010

NBC Parent Participation Workshops
Teachers' Guide to Television
699 Madison Avenue
New York, NY 10021

Action for Children's Television
46 Austin Street
Newtonville, MA 02160

National Council for Children and Television
20 Nassau Street
Princeton, NY 08540

Prime Time
120 LaSalle Street
Chicago, IL 60603

Videos
Black History: Lost, Stolen, or Strayed
Insight Media
2162 Broadway
New York, NY 10024
212-721-6316

I'll Fly Away
PBS Television Series
Washington Educational Television Association
Box 2636
Washington, DC 20009
703-998-2600

The Latino Family
Films for the Humanities & Science
P.O. Box 2053
Princeton, NJ 08543
609-275-1400

Partners Toward Achievement: A Home-School-Community Partnership
National Education Service
1252 Loesch Road
P.O. Box 8, Station T6
Bloomington, IN 47402-0008
812-336-7701

Shared Decision Making
Insight Media
2162 Broadway
New York, NY 10024
212-721-6316

The Status of Latina Women
Films for the Humanities & Science
P.O. Box 2053
Princeton, NJ 08543
609-275-1400
800-257-5126

Working with Parents: Home-School Collaboration
Insight Media
2162 Broadway
New York, NY 10024
212-721-6316

Web Sites

Brain-based Learning

Advanced Learning Concepts-Brain Gym Movements
www.globaldilog.com/-tez/alc/bgmove.htm

Brain-Flex: Independent Learning
www.com.au/-cbounds/Brain_Flex

The BrainTainment Center
world.brain.com

Funderstanding
www.funderstanding.com/brain.htm

Diversity Awareness

African American

African-American Resources
www.rain/org/-kmx/aa.html

NAACP
www.shoga.wwa.com/-desktop/naacp.html

National Urban League
www.nul.org

Hispanic/Latino

Azteca Web Page
www.azteca.net/azteca/

Chicano/Latino Net
www.latino.sscnet.ucla.edu

Informatica PR-NET
www.geocities.com/capitolhill

Latino Interest Site
www.latino.sscnet.ucla.edu/latinos.links.html

Native American

American Indian Movement
www.netgate.net/-jsd/AIMintro.html

Indian Defense League of America
www.tuscaroras.com/IDLA

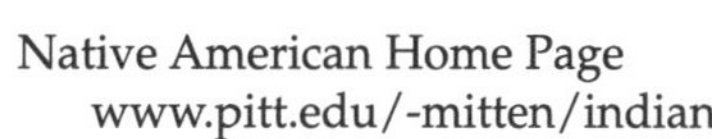

Native American Home Page
www.pitt.edu/-mitten/indians

Resources for Native American Families
www.familyvillage.wisc.edu/frc-natv.htm

Other Diversity Sites

Diversity Resources
www.siue.edu/jandris/htmldocuments/andric/diversity.html

National Center for Research on Cultural Diversity and Second Language Learning
zzyx.ucsc.edu/cntr/cntr.html

Pathways to Diversity on the World Wide Web
www.usc.edu/library/QF/diversity

Family Literacy

Family Literacy in Canada: Profiles of Effective Practices
www.nald.ca/fulltext/family/famlit/cover.htm

Family Literacy Foundation
www.read2kids.org/

The James Flanigan Foundation
www.lit4life.org/

Literacy Volunteers of America
www.literacyvolunteers.org

National Center for Family Literacy
www.famlit.org

National Institute for Literacy
novel.nifl.gov

National Institute on Early Childhood Development and Education
www.ed.gov/offices/OERI/ECI

Ohio Family Literacy Initiative
literacy.kent.edu/oasis/family/ohfamlit.html

U.S. Government Resources
www.ed.gov/family

Father Involvement

The American Family Network
www.customcpu.co:80/personal/mneligh/afn/links.htm

Dad and Son: Memoir
www.parentsplace.com/readroom/goodfathers/index.html

Dad Stuff
tam2000.tau.edu/-phayes/dad-stuf.html.

Fathering Issues and Resources
www.parentsplace.com/readroom/father.html

FatherNet Gopher
Gopher://finman.mes.umn.edu:80/11/FatherNet

Father's Resource Center
www.parentsplace.com/readroom/frc/index/html

Father's Rights and Equality Exchange
www.vix.com/free/

Father's Rights Foundation
www.intrnet/-risaacs/index.html

Life with Father
gertrude.artuiuc.edu/ludgate/the/place/place2.html

M.E.N. Magazine
www.vix.com/pub/men/index.html

San Diego Fathers' Group
ftp://ftp.cts.com/pub/jcb/fathers.html

Single Dad's Index
www.vix.com/pub/men/single-dad.html

Single Fathers
www.pitt.edu/-jsims/singlefa.html

General Reading Information

AskERIC
www.askeric.org/

ERIC Clearinghouse on Reading, English and Communication
www.indiana.edu/-eric_rec/

International Reading Association
www.reading.org

Parents and Children

Candlelight Stories
www.candlelightstories.com

Carol Hurst's Children's Literature Site
www.carolhurst.com

Children's Literature Web Guide
www.acs.ucalgary.ca/-dkbrown

Children's Storybooks Online
www.magickeys.com/books/index

Dragon Fly
www.muohio.edo/dragonfly

Eduplace
www.eduplace.com

Family Education Network
www.familyeducation.com

Family Planet
 www.familyplanet.com

The Family Web
 www.familyweb.com

Family World
 www.family.com

For and About Children
 www.ocsny.com/-mdm/children.html

Functional Family
 pubweb.acns.nwu.edu/-rab/hnhome1.htm

Kid Zone
 www.Idoline.org/Id-indepth/
 postsecondary/muskingham

Poetry for Kids
 www.nesbitt.com/poetry

Local Family Activities
 111.family.com

National Parent Information Network
 www.ericps.ed.uiuc.edu.npin

The National Parenting Center
 www.stpt.com/TNPC/

Parenting
 iquest.com/-jsm/moms/parenting.html

Parents as Teachers National Center
 www.patnc.org

Parents Helping Parents
 www.portal.com:80/-cbntmkr/php.html

Parents Place
 www.parentsplace.com

Parents Soup
 www.parentsoup.com

Positive Parenting Home Page
 www.fishnet.net/-pparents/

Reader's Theatre
 www.aaronshep.com

Save the Children
 www.winternet.com/-jannmart/nkcindex.html